Memories of War, Promises of Peace

Memories of War

Promises of Peace

Mary Jo Leddy

LESTER
&ORPEN
DENNYS
PUBLISHERS

Copyright ©1989, Mary Jo Leddy

All rights reserved. No part of this publication may be reproduced in any manner whatsoever without written permission from the Publisher, except by a reviewer who wishes to quote brief passages for inclusion in a review.

FIRST EDITION

Canadian Cataloguing in Publication Data
Leddy, Mary Joanna, 1946–
    Memories of War, Promises of Peace
ISBN 0-88619-254-4 (bound)   ISBN 0-88619-260-9 (pbk.)

1. Leddy, John Edward. 2. Leddy, Rita Theresa. 3. World War, 1939–1945– Europe. 4. World War, 1939–1945– Public Opinion. 5. World War, 1939–1945– Medical care. 6. Surgeons–Biography. 7. Peace. 8. Nurses–Biography. I. Title.

D811.5.L43   1989   940.54'75'0922   C89-094174-2

The Publisher wishes to acknowledge the assistance of the Ontario Arts Council.

Printed and bound in Canada by
T. H. Best Printing Company Limited

Lester & Orpen Dennys Limited
78 Sullivan Street
Toronto, Canada M5T 1C1

*In memory of
Cam Willis, Cherub Laidlaw, Ted Slack, Johnny Boles,
and all of those
who now rely on others
to share the memories of war*

Acknowledgements

Because this book is essentially a work of gratitude, it seems most appropriate to acknowledge those who made it possible.

In the initial stages of preparing the research of this manuscript, Zoria Sirman typed and photocopied the memories of Jack and Rita Leddy with her usual competence and personal care. The staff (particularly Pat Munroe) of the medical records library at St. Paul's Hospital were very helpful at this time.

Jack Costello SJ offered several perceptive comments as this text was being written. My sister, Jennifer Leddy, reviewed the entire manuscript and offered invaluable suggestions. The computer upon which this manuscript was written was generously donated by Dr. Carole Rittner RSM. I am especially grateful to the Sisters of Our Lady of Sion on Oakmount Road for the support and encouragement which they gave to me and to my family during the difficult months in which this book was written.

My agent, Lee Davis Creal (of the Lucinda Vardey Agency), was instrumental in making the idea of this book a concrete possibility. Louise Dennys and Malcolm Lester have been most gracious as publishers. Gena Gorrell, senior editor at Lester & Orpen Dennys, brought her considerable expertise to bear on the final draft of the text.

It would not have been possible for me to take the time to write this book without the generous financial assistance of the Ontario Arts Council.

Most of all, thanks to Mom and Dad, more than I can say.

Memories of War, Promises of Peace

CONTENTS

CHAPTER I
An Introduction   1

CHAPTER II
Sounds of a Distant War   11

CHAPTER III
"For Better or Worse, in Good Times and in Bad"   25

CHAPTER IV
The First Farewell   37

CHAPTER V
Crossings   53

CHAPTER VI
Neither Here nor There   75

CHAPTER VII
"The Sickly Sweet Smell of Death"   93

CHAPTER VIII
Stitches in Time   113

CHAPTER IX
Small Victories   137

Epilogue: A World of Difference   153

Notes   171

I

An Introduction

It was a closed book—or so it seemed. We knew it was up there, in the attic, somewhere in Dad's old war trunk. The yellow pages of his diary were fading like the half-forgotten era of the Second World War.

Then came the time of remembering.

As the house that had been our home began to empty out, the weight of what was up there in the attic seemed to press down on the rooms of our more conscious life below. My parents became more aware of the things that belonged not so much to their three children as to them. It was not that Dad had forgotten completely about his war diary or about what he and Mom had lived through during those years. There were just so many other things to keep in mind—the demands of a medical practice, the responsibility for a hospital, children and grandchildren who exerted undeniable claims for time and attention. Life seemed to have picked them up after the war and thrown them forward along a path that left them little time to retrace their steps to the point from which they had started to journey together.

Then came the year when my father began to move through life more slowly. A bad back made it increasingly difficult for him to stride along the fairways of the golf course on his days off. He could no longer stand for the hours of intense concentration required by major surgery. Mom slowed to keep pace beside him—where she had always been.

Then came the day when Dad went up the stairs to the attic and brought down the tattered old diary. It was on one of the few occasions when I had returned from Toronto to visit them at home in Saskatoon. I was only mildly interested in the story that he began to page through, carefully separating the leaves of paper so that whatever was binding them together would not fall apart.

There were other stories I was more involved in at the time. As a journalist, I had visited war-torn areas of the world such as Lebanon and had interviewed people caught up in the conflicts of Central America. Here in Canada, I was spilling a lot of ink in the process of writing the stories of people whose lives were given over to the struggle for justice and peace.

My parents' story seemed more familiar, even prosaic. As I was growing up it had come out in bits and pieces, on the run and by the way.

It went something like this—or so I thought: They had been married in Toronto after the war broke out. He had gone overseas as a young doctor in a M.A.S.H.-like unit and had worked in Normandy, Belgium, and Holland. She had found a way of being nearer to him by volunteering to nurse in England. The war had ended and I had been born—the period at the end of that particular sentence.

Somehow, I grew up thinking that their real story began with mine. This wasn't only childish self-centredness on my part. It was also the way they usually interpreted the course of their life together. The birth of their first child had been the sign of everything promising in life, after their years of struggling to mitigate the death and destruction of war.

I watched as Dad turned the pages of his diary—deliberately, for he is a deliberate man, but with some delicacy. Tears began to form in the corners of his eyes. I had seen those tears before, when, as a child, I had gone with him to the cenotaph ceremonies on Remembrance Day in Saskatoon. They were the only tears he never hid from us, tears that I sensed—even then—I could not wipe away.

The pages turned, one after the other. Occasionally he would chuckle and smile, and then he would get that intent look which we always associated with the serious business of surgery. He seemed very far away as he sat there in his old chair in the den, looking through—and beyond—the pages.

From somewhere in between my feelings of being either a little girl or an old woman, I reached out and asked Dad if I could read his diary. Sure, he said, sure.

He had always been a sureness in my life. Yet I was unsure what I would find in his diary. He had never, as long as I had known him, been given to writing down his personal thoughts and reflections. Medical reports, case studies, and business letters were more his style. His feelings were set down in action. He was what he did—the way he touched, the way he moved. He revealed himself in his operating, his golfing, and his dancing. Writing in a diary seemed out of character for a man who was such an open book.

It would have been so much more like my mother, who was more poetry than prose. She loved to curl up with a good book and would linger over lines of poetry between loads of laundry. We looked forward to nights when she would tell us stories of faraway places and of the friendly little folk who danced on our walls when the full moon beamed through the windows of our bedroom. Her correspondence was extensive and every day letters would arrive for her from all over the world. In parish groups and women's organizations, she was much in demand as the writer of funny skits and plays for every occasion. Mom was the one we knew through her words—the way she felt them, how she gave them forth and when she gathered them into herself. As a teenager she had written in the utmost confidence to "Dear Diary", but she had never kept anything resembling a diary during the war.

I opened Dad's book. It took some time before I could decipher his handwriting. His strokes of the pen were like the marks of his life—swift, condensed. There were marginal notes, sketches of arteries and bones, points about amputation and "irreversible shock". And then there were lines I could begin to relate to:

> *Oct. 19/41, Halifax* In spite of a certain carefree spirit, there is also another feeling, one of apprehension, tension, and a strange melancholy.
>
> *Sept. 30/42, crossing the Atlantic* I have been lying in my bunk waiting for supper—just looking at your pictures in my wallet, Rita. They help a lot.
>
> *Sept. 29/43, England* Great news! Rita is coming over in a few weeks. Am thrilled.
>
> *July 23/44, Normandy* Worrying about Rita—many flying bombs going over to England.... It has just occurred to me—we have been shelled! bombed! machine-gunned! mines all around us! Some war!
>
> *August/44, Normandy* Men dying like flies.
>
> *May 5/45* Sitting by the dock at Ostend waiting to push off for England and for Rita.
>
> *May 8/45* VE Day! Saw Rita in Birmingham.

October 22/45—Rita's birthday We are expecting Junior in February 1946.

Tears welled within me. I had seen enough in these scant entries to know that there was much more between the lines. There was a love story, a tale of quiet courage and of a young couple's searing encounter with the reality of war. I had read enough to know that it was also, somehow, my story. The dates of the diary entries made it clear that I had been conceived in England on or about VE Day.

Our lives are often far deeper and longer than we know. For years I have been committed to the peace movement in any number of ways. When people asked me how I had arrived at such convictions, I used to answer that one had only to learn about the facts of life and death in the nuclear age. If we had more time to talk, I would refer to some of the values my parents had taught me, or to the lessons I had learned while studying the history of the Holocaust at university. It had never occurred to me to begin with my own beginning, with the fact of my own life. Now I realize that I began in a moment of passionate longing for peace—in a moment of promise.

There was so much more I wanted and needed to understand after I had finished the diary that I asked Mom and Dad if they would try to write down their experiences during the war. They were not sure it was worth the time and effort. I was sure it was, very sure.

It took them most of a year. Dad approached his task as conscientiously as if he were preparing for a major operation. He summoned up all the details he could remember and double-checked them in history books and medical journals. All of this was dictated into a machine, for transcribing. Mom's memories seemed to flow more easily, as if she were telling me a bedtime story about people in a distant and darkened land.

Through these two memories of war, I discovered anew the story of Jack Leddy and Rita Wilkinson. It is a story that is understated, now as then. Yet it is all the more compelling in its simplicity, the more romantic in its reserve. I met them for the first time fifty years ago, when they were young and oh, so in love—two people not yet my parents, two people much younger than I am now. They were tender and brave and true to each other. Fun to be with, they were fabulously, recklessly generous with their lives. Spirit, that's the word that comes to mind—they lived with spirit and made a spirited response to the times that were theirs. It was more than the spirit of youth, although it was that too. There was something that inspired them, turned them inside out, and called them beyond themselves—to each other and beyond each other. Jack and Rita cared for the world as much as they cared for each other.

I liked them a lot. I thought that we could have been friends then, that we could be friends now.

These were two young people who had promised each other the future. At times it seemed as if that was all they had left to give to each other—and even that could be taken away. Yet it was a promise they kept despite the months and years of separation exacted by the war. Jack and Rita wrote each other every day that they could not be together. Every day—rain or shine, raid or no raid.[1] They were separated by an ocean at times, by the Channel at other times, and always by the needs of the human beings who depended on their care and competence for one more chance at life. But every day two letters were mailed, one to Rita Leddy and the other to Jack Leddy. Promises of love.

Every now and then, my brother and sister and I used to catch a glimpse of the extended romance between Jack and Rita as they danced cheek to cheek in the living room to an old Glenn Miller record. As teenagers, we thought they were getting a little old for all that. Our observations were ignored, just as they had shrugged off the advice of those who told them they were too young to go off to war and "all that". Only recently have I realized how dancing was their most delightful act of defiance, a refusal to limp away from war.

As I caught the romantic strain of their memories, the noises of war sounded all the more loudly: the putt-putt of the buzz bomb, the seconds of silence before it fell, the moans of the wounded as they were carried into the operating room, and then, sometimes, silence again. Rita and Jack listened to all of this, and more. They saw the mangled bodies, the rotting flesh, the faces frozen in terror, the eyes fixed in the stare of death. For years they helped to pick up the human pieces of war.

War appears more acceptable when it is seen "from above"—from afar or years later. History books about the Second World War are often written from this perspective in order to situate the welter of events within a certain context. Such a perspective invites debates about just and unjust wars, discussions about successes and failures, descriptions of winners and losers. It is an important but dangerously incomplete perspective.

The story of Jack and Rita provides a different view of the reality of war, a ground-level view. From this perspective, war is seen in terms of cruelty and compassion, of commission and omission, of senseless suffering and meaningful sacrifice. At this level, war registers as a profit for a few and a loss for many. Jack and Rita had picked up too many of the casualties of war not to count its cost.

We may know almost all the facts about the Second World War but we will probably never know the whole truth, the whole story. Perhaps all we have is what philosopher Hannah Arendt called "moments of truth", stories that reveal, however briefly, something of what it was all about.

The story of Jack and Rita has been a moment of truth for me, and it may be so for others. In a way it is a very Canadian story—simply transparent, suffused with its own splendid light. Jack and Rita's experience bears little resemblance either to that of the countless victims of the war or to that of those who were the victimizers. Neither heroes nor villains, they remained life-size in a time diminished by terror.

As I talked to Mom and Dad about their memories, I heard them say again and again that they considered themselves to be among the fortunate ones. The war had cost them only a period of their lives, years of marriage, and the energy of youth. There were some dreams they could no longer afford. Yet, if they have fewer hopes now, they have even fewer regrets. They believe that they helped to make a small difference between war and peace.

This is a true story about that difference—which is all the difference in the world.

II

Sounds of a Distant War

September 10, 1939, began as an unusually warm autumn morning in the small Saskatchewan town where Jack Leddy had just opened his medical practice. It became a special afternoon in Oshawa, Ontario for a large Irish clan of relatives who gathered to see Rita Wilkinson, one of their own, off to university. It was also the day on which Canada declared war against Germany.

In the fall of 1939, Jack Leddy was working as a general practitioner in Delisle, Saskatchewan. On the morning of September 10, he had gone to Sunday mass with his landlady, Mrs. Gezy. She was a warm-hearted woman of German descent who had opened her home and her heart to the young doctor, who had recently returned to the prairies from medical school in the east. It was at church that they learned that Canada had joined the war.

■

Mrs. Gezy started to cry when the priest announced that Canada had declared war on Germany. She sat there with tears rolling down her cheeks. She turned to me and said, "So many young Canadian boys and so many German boys will die because of Hitler starting this war."

I walked home with her, kicking the sand as I walked along.

There was a lot of sand to kick around in Delisle at that time. The town was just coming out of the Depression. For most of the people on the prairies, survival had been a major achievement during the thirties. Many had seen their land and their future drift by the side of the road during the dust-bowl era. However, in the fall of 1939 they were having their first good crop in years. Finally they had reason to celebrate. At harvest time, the people gathered to help each other bring in the crops and then they sat down together to a table where the food stretched as far as the arm could reach. Invariably, the young doctor found himself sitting next to someone's daughter.

■

As a single man of 26 years of age, I had to be pretty nimble to dodge the older women who acted as marriage brokers. They were always finding ways and means of inviting me to the fowl dinners where there was a young lady as a guest. But I kept going because the food was so good!

When the hunting season opened on the prairies Jack took advantage of numerous invitations to go duck shooting. It was the only time in his life that he enjoyed going on a shoot. After the war, when his friends invited him to go hunting with them, he always refused. He said he had lost interest in killing—even ducks.

■

> I had the opportunity to do a little shooting with some of the local farmers, the lumber yard foreman, and the bank manager. They were all crack shots. I loved rising in the early morning to catch the duck shooting, and the stubble shoots when the ducks came in to feed later on in the afternoon. My companions always bagged more than I did but it didn't matter. The fellowship was great.

For Jack and the other three hundred people in Delisle, the war seemed very distant indeed. After Hitler's invasion of Poland, there was a lull in military action for several months. Jack was less interested in the politics of Europe than in the politics of small-town life on the prairies.

■

> Never having lived in a small town, I was struck by how everyone seemed to know everyone else's business. But they also knew how to co-exist and there was always someone around who seemed to be able to control the inevitable bickering and gossip that developed from time to time....

> There was a group of farmers in the area who were considered quite left-wing at the time. They had come through the dirty 30s with the conviction that there should be another party (other than the Liberals and Conservatives) to make it possible for people of ordinary means to avoid poverty should another depression happen.

Jack had grown up in Saskatoon, the larger city not too far from Delisle. It was a peaceful settlement on the banks of the South Saskatchewan River. The major threats to its existence came from the forces of nature—from the dangers which the wind, hail, and blistering sun posed to the crops. Stories were told of those who had been lost in blinding blizzards and of children who had been sucked into the swirling currents of the river. Yet once, some twenty-five years earlier, there had been signs of a different kind of threat.

■

> My brother Frances and I heard trains rumbling at night across the old CPR bridge near our house. We would lie in bed and listen. We knew the trains were carrying soldiers over to the war. We had seen the soldiers in their uniforms on the streets and had asked what they were doing and where they were going. I can't remember exactly what they said but I knew they were going to war. I was five or six at the time.

Like most of the children in Saskatoon, Jack grew up thinking that the First World War was the war to end all wars. In 1934 he took part in an undergraduate debate at the University of Saskatchewan in which it was resolved to abolish the Canadian Officer Training Corps as a credit class. Jack was on the winning side of the debate.

■

I argued strongly against the Canadian Officer Training Corps being a credit class. I couldn't see the point in this snap class which I thought was just a way for some people to get money by parading around periodically. It didn't seem fair when all of us were having a hard time during the Depression. Besides...we all thought there would never be another war.

Some of my best friends in Saskatoon were of German descent but we didn't really talk about Hitler. On the few times that we did, they said that he was doing something good for the economy of Germany but there was nothing anyone else should worry about. I certainly wasn't interested in the aspirations of Adolf Hitler at that time. There were better things to do—like playing hockey and going to dances.

However, the aspirations of Adolf Hitler had become more of a concern by the time Jack went to medical school at McGill University in Montreal. Although his studies consumed most of his time, there were moments when the reality of what was happening in Europe claimed his attention.

■

Our fraternity house on Pine Avenue decided to have a debate every Saturday afternoon before watching the football game. One of the debates in 1937 was "Will there ever be a war with Nazi Germany or is this not at all possible?" As the debate swung back and forth, I quoted from *Inside Europe* by John Gunther to show that there was a real danger of war with Germany. Other members of the frat thought that the Germans could not afford a war economically.

War with Germany had become a real but not a pressing danger as Jack began to establish himself as a country doctor in Delisle. The Bentley family, who were always talking about their two sons in major-league hockey, helped him get some of the furniture and equipment he needed. He set up his office in the den of Mrs. Gezy's large house; from the window of that room, he could look out and see the wheat fields rippling on for miles. A real horse-and-buggy doctor, Jack would hitch up the mare and drive out to visit those who were too sick to come in from the farms.

If 1939 marks the beginning of the time when my father's story was altered by the history of the Second World War, Delisle marks the spot where his own ground became more firm beneath him. His feet never really left that ground. He was a prairie boy with a clear horizon of being that not even the war could ever fully obscure.

Jack could stand out on the prairie, as he had as a child, and see how the land gave way so graciously to the sky. Those of us who were planted in this horizon grew up seeing, above all, the sky—because there was so little else to get in the way. As the land went to sleep, the sky began to awaken within us. Scrunching along in our snow boots on the way home from school, we were stopped in our tracks at the sight of the pink—the colour that suffuses the sky on the evening before a snowfall. The transformation of our cold and white world into a place of gentle light took our breath away. At night we saw by more than moonlight. The Northern Lights shimmered like souls sending glimmers of grace to those below.

As darkness began to fall over Europe, the young doctor on the prairies was often wakened by a phone ringing through the night. The voice at the other end of the line would say it was an emergency. Jack would run to get Eddie Nugent, who would take him over the frozen fields in a horse-drawn sleigh. The sky would stretch long before them.

Eddie Nugent was one of the young boys from Delisle who would be killed in the distant war.

On the afternoon of September 10, 1939, all the cousins had been invited over to Aunt May's house on Division Street in Oshawa for a send-off party for "little Rita". Rita had just graduated from her RN course at St. Michael's Hospital in Toronto and had come home for a break. The next day she would be returning to Toronto to begin a graduate course in nursing at the university.

The cousins began piling onto the veranda of the slightly sagging house where Rita and her three older brothers had grown up. The brothers arrived with their women in tow. Wives and girlfriends knew this was a command performance, because the Wilkinson boys adored their baby sister.

Rita settled into her place of honour on the porch railing—and almost fell off as her charming brothers began to regale the gathering with family stories: about how Grandma Quigley used to hang her bloomers on the line in a pillowcase so the neighbours wouldn't see them; about the times little Rita and her friend Bernice Higgins used to sneak into the church in the afternoons and preach sermons from the pulpit to the empty pews.

A bottle of whisky was brought out to celebrate the occasion. There was the usual toast to Aunt Betty, to her beauty and her continued good fortune. She had married Harry Hatch from Napanee and they had put some of their Irish talents to good use during Prohibition—coming out of it with their company, Hiram Walker Distilleries, profitably established. Then followed the usual solemn toast to Uncle Henry, the only priest in the clan, and to all the priests of Holy Mother the Church. Finally someone proposed an irreverent toast to General Motors, the company which had graced Oshawa with its grimy presence. Things were getting better at General Motors and therefore in Oshawa. The strikes and layoffs which had been so much a part of the Depression were becoming less frequent by the fall of 1939.

The conversation turned ever so briefly to Canada's declaration of war, which had been announced earlier that day on the radio. Two of Rita's brothers had little sympathy for the plight of the English and expounded their fervent belief that it was stupid for anyone to go and help the "limeys". Rita didn't bother arguing with them that afternoon and kept her thoughts to herself. She had heard about what had happened to the Jews in Germany in the rampage of destruction on *Kristallnacht* and she just didn't think that was any way to treat people.

Rita's mother came out and called everyone to the table—a call that seemed far more urgent and important than any war.

It was only when Rita was sitting in the lecture hall at the University of Toronto a few days later that the significance of the news of the war began to dawn on her. The autumn sun was flooding through the windows as the nurses made small talk while they waited for the instructor to appear. They discovered that they came from all over Canada, the United States, and several other countries as well. This was their first class in the post-graduate course in Teaching and Supervision.

The Director of the School of Nursing entered the classroom and introduced herself as Miss Kathleen Russell. She was a gracious and gentle lady in late middle age. She came right to the point: "Good morning, ladies. Today we are starting the academic year. I hope that you will enjoy your time at the school. Our country is at war. We shall have our worries about our loved ones who may be leaving to join the forces. The news from Europe is bad. Let us hope and pray that before this academic year is finished the war will be over."

Rita had been born at the end of the First World War and had little sense of what war could mean in reality—but she thought it was important to find out. She went to the library to find everything she could on Hitler and the Nazis and then returned to her room in the residence of St. Michael's Hospital to read. Much of this information was news to Rita. Her years of training had been so totally engaging that the reports of the problems of Europe had seemed pale in comparison to the fascinating day-to-day developments in the life of a hospital.

A hospital is a whole world in itself with its particular share of joys, sufferings, and struggles. We were completely absorbed in that world and didn't think about what was going on outside of the hospital. We studied, worked on wards, and lived for days off.

The world of the hospital was almost as complete as the tightly knit Irish-Catholic world which had encompassed her childhood. St. Gregory's Parish and School in Oshawa had provided a focus for all the fervour and frivolity of Rita's growing years. It was a vibrant community shaped by loyalties to family and to friends. Keeping the faith meant being faithful to people.

Rita's life was rooted in these close relationships. It was in this community of people that she flourished and branched forth. In due season she became friends with a few of the Protestant kids in the public high school she attended, and with the Jewish boy who lived on her street. Some of her brothers began to wonder if there was any limit to her loyalties.

> In my last year of high school, I went to parties with the rabbi's son. His name was Nathan Tessis, a bright and happy person and the only Jew I had ever really met. Later, in the spring of 1940, I ran into him at the University of Toronto while I was walking through the campus. He was not the happy boy I had known in Oshawa. By that time we were hearing about some of the things Hitler was doing to the Jews in Germany and I knew it was on his mind.

It was no longer possible to ignore the things happening in the world outside St. Gregory's Parish and the School of Nursing. The months of the so-called "Phony War" were over, and the news from Europe was shocking. By the summer of 1940 the German army had invaded Denmark and Norway and, in the lightning strike of the *Blitzkrieg*, had overrun the Low Countries and much of France. British troops in France had been cornered at Dunkirk, and had only barely been saved by a vast flotilla of boats, large and small, that crossed the Channel to pluck the men off the coast.

As she listened to the news of the rescue at Dunkirk, Rita was filled with admiration for the valiant men and women who had risked their lives out of loyalty to people they did not know at all.

Rita finished her year at the University of Toronto and after graduation went back to St. Michael's to become the supervisor of the men's surgical ward. On Sunday afternoons in the summer, she would often take the bus home for another family gathering at their home on Division Street. All the serious burdens of work seemed to lift with the lightness of the Wilkinson and Carr laughter. Rita's brothers had learned that they could joke with her about almost anything—except "the limeys".

The summer of 1940 was also a season of change for Jack Leddy in Delisle. By that time, he had been able to send some money home to help his parents and younger brothers and sisters, and now seemed the moment to continue his training to become a surgeon. He accepted the offer of a job as resident surgeon at St. Michael's Hospital in Toronto. There were many farewell parties for the young, still unmarried doctor who had become so much a part of daily life in Delisle.

He left Delisle a few pounds heavier than when he had arrived. As he sat enjoying one of his last turkey dinners in that little town, one of the old ladies sidled up to him and said, "You'll make someone a fine catch."

III

*"For Better or Worse,
in Good Times and in Bad"*

Rita Wilkinson and Jack Leddy entered each other's worlds in the fall of 1940 as he made his rounds on the men's surgical ward at St. Michael's. She detected that the tall, thin doctor from the west was having a hard time adjusting to a large teaching hospital. She also noticed what he was wearing.

I felt sorry for him and yet I enjoyed teasing him. I asked him if he had bought his ties in Delisle? And wherever did he get such strange looking shoes—at old man Bentley's shop in Delisle? I knew Jack took me seriously when he ran to his room to change his tie when I didn't approve. One day he said to me, "Well, why don't you show me something better?" So we went shopping together over at Eaton's on Yonge St.

Rita and Jack's paths began to cross more frequently. Sometimes it was between classes—his lectures on surgery to the nurses were followed by classes on surgical nursing by Rita. At other times they would chat as they examined the charts at the nursing station on the ward: What do you think about this blood pressure? What's the latest news from the war? What do you do on nights off?

During the Christmas break, Jack went to New York with his friend Jim Emmett to dance the nights away to the music of Glenn Miller and Sammy Kaye. They had a wonderful time walking around Times Square and going to night clubs. But when Jack returned to Toronto, he couldn't remember any of the girls he had danced with. He was much more intrigued by the young nursing supervisor whom he now called "Beany". He hadn't taken her dancing, not yet, but he had seen her work and was impressed.

■

> She was very pretty and a great favourite of George Wilson, the crusty old Chief of Surgery. Most of his surgical staff followed him around meek as sheep because they knew that if they didn't jump when he commanded they would be removed from the team. He seemed to like Rita because she spoke up to him, politely, when he was cross—which was most of the time. And she could make him laugh. She was very dedicated to her work, putting in long hours for little pay, and she was very efficient. Everything was well organized and ready for rounds every day.
>
> I noticed that she always defended the nurses under her and was ready to help the student nurses with their problems. She showed great respect for the patients under her care—patients whom others

found difficult to respect. Her ward was a "public ward" of men who were unable to pay for their hospitalization. Many of them were winos who had been found in the alleys off Queen Street. Rita had to take their bottles and cigarettes away from them at night so they wouldn't set the place on fire.

These patients were the cases which we young doctors and nurses examined in order to learn more about surgery. I could see that Rita became very upset with us when we weren't sensitive to the fact that these derelicts were people with feelings, with personal and family problems of their own.

However, Rita's criticisms were far easier to take than those of the brilliant but temperamental George Wilson. The Chief of Surgery was tough on the young doctor from the prairies who had the arrogance to think he could become a resident without first having a few years of working experience in a hospital.

■

I knew I had to get up pretty early in the morning to get to the wards before Doctor Wilson arrived at the hospital. I would get up at 6:00 a.m. and go around the wards to check on the patients, particularly those who had arrived as emergencies the night before. Dr. Wilson would arrive at 7:30 a.m. and demand a complete report on all the new patients. He ran a very tight ship. I didn't like this discipline and found it very hard to accept after having been my own boss in general practice. But I came to see it as necessary. When you are involved in making life-and-death decisions every day, it is important to be able to work as a disciplined team, to follow orders as well as to give them.

During the early eighties, I used to pass St. Michael's almost every day as I rode the Queen streetcar to and from the office of *Catholic New Times*. My own journey through life had led me to work in a building only a few blocks from the hospital where my parents had met in 1940 and where I had been born in 1946. The Victoria Street stop, on the Humber–Neville streetcar line, always gave me reason to pause.

As I looked out of the window from my seat, the hospital building began to appear as a stone marker of the place where my parents had discovered not only each other but also their vocation in life.

Their vocation to heal was much more than a job, a career, or a profession. It was who they were, and why and how. It was something they could no more not do than not be themselves. It meant that the call of a suffering person became an imperative for them. Their lives were claimed by such calls. These claims seemed to leave them with not less but more of a sense of themselves.

Somehow, somewhere, Mom and Dad also came to terms with the inherent limitations of their response to such a calling. They knew that the moment when life began and the moment when it ended were beyond them. Yet they also believed that they could do something in those moments in between, when people needed a little assistance to live a little longer, to live a little better.

As their daughter, I grew into a sense that one's life could be called upon and claimed. I learned that, although one could not respond to everything in life, one could still do something.

Rita could not help but admire Jack's steadiness and decisiveness under pressure. Yet he was more than a little unsettling. She was used to going to concerts and plays with her other boyfriends but Jack usually wanted to go to a hockey game or a wrestling match at Maple Leaf Gardens. He was brash in comparison to some of the elegant and charming men she had been dating. As for Jack, he didn't understand what she saw in them.

◾

> There were about five other fellows on staff who were anxious to take Rita out. I was annoyed when she couldn't go out with me one weekend because she was "booked". On Monday, I told her to "dust off" those other fellows if she ever expected to marry me. I can only say that I got told off for my arrogance—but good. She said, "Who do you think you are—what's so special about you?" I apologized—at least I think I did.

Yet Rita was evidently starting to think there was something special about Jack.

> Although the war was constantly on our minds, we managed to have some good times. All of us were working long hours and leisure time was limited. In the evening, Jack and I would sometimes walk along the streets around the hospital. We would often talk about the war. He had planned on continuing his surgical training but now he wasn't so sure. It was a time of uncertainty for all of us.

During late 1940 and early 1941 the news from Europe seemed to grow worse every day. Italy, Hungary, Bulgaria, and Romania had all joined the German cause, and Yugoslavia and Greece had been conquered. With war raging in North Africa, the Mediterranean and the Suez Canal seemed likely to fall under German control. Meanwhile, the Battle of Britain raged in the skies: London was being bombed and there were constant reports of the civilian casualties of the blitz. The young nurses and doctors read the newspapers during their meal breaks; staff gathered in clusters to listen to Churchill's speeches on the radio and marvelled at the courage of the British. The impossible thought began to cross their minds— would England be invaded? The war began to intrude on the self-enclosed world of the hospital. Patients spoke about sons or daughters who had moved away from home to join in the war effort in some way. There was hardly anyone on staff who hadn't heard of some relative or friend going overseas. Some of the younger nurses left to join the forces, and older nurses, who had not worked in years, returned to floor duty to take their place. Interns and residents were faced with important questions about their futures—would they remain at the hospital to continue their training or would they join the armed forces and leave their training until after the war? And there were other, more personal decisions to be made.

We had a big party at the end of the intern year in the late spring of 1941. It was a grand event at the Royal York Hotel and we all made an extra effort to dress for the occasion. We were trying so hard to have a wonderful time—because our group was breaking up. So many of the doctors and nurses were joining the forces.

> True to form, Jack didn't choose a romantic spot—or the right moment to propose to me. We were walking across the parking lot of the hotel on our return to the hospital. He just said it—simple and fast—"Let's get married." It seems I must have said yes.

Jack had also made a decision, although not a highly motivated decision, to join the army. He knew that several of the other doctors were considering this and it just seemed the right thing to do. There was also a lot of pressure from some of the older doctors who had been in the First World War. "Now it's your turn," they told the younger doctors. Dr. Wilson, who had served in Gallipoli during the First World War, would stride along the hospital corridors whistling, "There'll Always Be an England". The veteran doctors stressed the particular need for anyone with even partial surgical training. Jack knew that he had all the requirements: He was twenty-eight, still single, and in first-class health—and he did have some training in surgery.

It had become apparent by then that the war was going to last a lot longer than had been anticipated. Still, Jack checked out some other options.

■

> Although I felt that I would probably be going into the army, I still thought that there was a possibility that there would be enough younger doctors who would join and that the rest of us would not be needed. So I went over to the Banting Institute where I met William Boyd, the great doctor who was the Chief Pathologist at the Institute. He was considered one of the finest teachers in Canada and, in fact, in the world. I told him that I was thinking

of joining the army but that, if I didn't, I would be interested in furthering my surgical training. I asked him if he would take me on as a resident in Pathology. He said that he had many applicants but that he would be glad to accept me for a position in July. I was very flattered and looked forward to joining him at the Institute.

However, I discussed the matter with Rita and she said, "Well, I know we are engaged and you want to stay here in Canada but I also know you feel you should join the army—so perhaps you should tell Dr. Boyd that for this reason you won't be able to accept his kind offer."

When Jack joined the Royal Canadian Army Medical Corps on July 1, 1941, the war in North Africa was going very badly for the Allied forces and it looked as if the Nazis were moving closer to realizing their dream of world domination. On his last day at the hospital, he went to see Dr. Wilson—who was delighted that Jack might eventually be going to England.

■

As I was going out the door, I turned and walked back to him and said, "Do you think I will ever be able to get an FRCS and become a surgeon?" He was always a rather taciturn individual so I was not surprised when he walked over to the window, stood with his hands behind his back, and looked out for what seemed a rather long time to me.

Then he walked back to me and said, "Yes, you can become a surgeon—I think you can, I think you will." This bucked me up considerably because I had been through a rough time with his demanding ways. As I stood waiting for his answer I had been almost sure he would tell me that I would never make a very good surgeon.

Jack began his basic training in Ottawa and then returned to Toronto on August 2 to get married. It was a simple morning service at the small chapel of the Basilian Fathers on St. Mary Street, with only a few friends and relatives present. Fr. Henry Carr witnessed the exchange of vows between his niece and her Jack. They promised to accept each other "for better or worse" and to be faithful "in good times and in bad".

IV

The First Farewell

Halifax was the place where Jack and Rita came to their own convictions about their involvement in the war effort. The young couple moved there almost immediately after their wedding, as Jack had been assigned to the Cogswell Street Military Hospital. He expected he would be there for only a short time before being sent overseas. In fact, almost a year would pass before his ship left Bedford Basin for England.

Halifax was teeming with people from all over the world who were waiting to be shipped over to one of the fronts. The housing capacity of the city had been stretched to its limits and the only home the young couple could find was a single room for ten dollars a week at Miss Jessie Beattie's on Jubilee Road. It was, as Jack recalls, "one hell of a dump".

Their greatest challenge was finding a place to eat in one of the crowded restaurants in the city. It was their first experience of queuing for the necessities of existence—queuing would become a way of life for most civilians in war-stricken areas. Jack and Rita got to know most of the greasy spoons in town.

One of their biggest treats was to stroll along Jubilee Road and get a slice off a turkey and make two enormous sandwiches.

In the mornings, Rita would walk with Jack over Citadel Hill on the way to the hospital. From the top of the hill, they could see the ships waiting in line to sail out from Bedford Basin and across the Atlantic—convoys of freighters, merchant ships, and troop transports taking part in the massive effort to get men, food, and equipment over to England. A ship would pass every three or four minutes. One day Jack and Rita counted thirty ships in a line stretching out to the Atlantic Ocean, with RCAF Catalina flying boats heading out to sea looking for U-boats.

Halifax was a city living on the edge of war.

■

> There was a certain carefree spirit in the city with so many young men milling around. But there was also another feeling—one of apprehension, tension, and a strange melancholy. It was worse at some times than at others—worse on bleak, cold, and rainy nights, worse after a convoy of troopships left for overseas. By then we knew that some of those ships would not be coming back. There were many freighters and transports torpedoed by the German submarines that were attempting to control the Atlantic in an effort to cut off the supply lines to Europe.

The people of Halifax had good reason to be apprehensive. The newspapers continued to report the seemingly invincible advance of the German forces, who were moving into Russia and quickly gaining ground in North Africa. Haligonians knew that the losses in Atlantic shipping were already enormous, and they were afraid that the war would come even closer to home. In conversations at the hospital, Jack heard about some of their fears.

■

> They expected the war to visit them soon. Perhaps in the form of the Germans shelling the port which was so important to the supply effort. Perhaps in the form of suicide bombers flying in from an aircraft carrier to bomb the ammunition dumps which were only six miles from Halifax.

After they moved to a second rooming-house—Mrs. F.W. Budd's on Waegwoltic Avenue—Rita heard of other apprehensions. The family was friendly with the author Hugh MacLennan, who had just written *Barometer Rising*, a book focusing on the Halifax explosion in 1917. Everyone in Halifax was talking about that dreadful day when over 1,600 people had died and a tenth of the city had been devastated after a steamer collided with a French munitions carrier. As the people of Halifax looked at the ships moving constantly in and out of Bedford Basin, they wondered whether the same kind of catastrophe would happen again.

The explosion of 1917 was the only time a Canadian city had directly experienced the effects of a world war. Halifax had its own memory of war.

Rita had not applied for a job in a hospital because they were not sure when Jack would be shipping out. It was the first time in her life she had had so much time on her hands and there were moments when she felt restless. She joined the library. She also began exploring the city after she left Jack at the hospital in the morning.

> I could see that Halifax would be a lovely place to live in peacetime. The Haligonians were overwhelmed with the influx of service people. For some of them this was the opportunity to make extra money but for the most part they were friendly and patient with the crowds. We were seeing Halifax at its worst but then they were seeing us at less than our best. We were young, impatient, and homesick, and anxious about the future. All of the young men, including Jack, were excited about going overseas and yet frightened too.

One of the places she visited was the house where Lucy Maud Montgomery had lived when she was attending college. As a young girl, Rita had loved reading *Anne of Green Gables* and had waited eagerly for each of the books that followed after it. Years later, Rita had become quite friendly with Montgomery's son Stuart when he was a young doctor at St. Michael's. From him she had learned about some of the struggles in Lucy Maud's rather sad life.

> I felt very close to Anne. She had such an imagination and I loved her original ways. I was puzzled how Lucy Maud was able to write such a delightful book in the midst of her very difficult life. But then, our life was getting more difficult.... I was glad to be able to imagine other times and places when war was not so real.

The war was becoming more real for Jack as he began treating some of the casualties of war.

■

A number of patients under my care had been through Dunkirk and Narvik. They were part of the Merchant Navy and they had taken part in rescuing the retreating British Army from Dunkirk and the men from the commando raids on Narvik, Norway. There were other gallant men who had risked their lives time and time again on the ships carrying supplies and arms to Britain. Some of them had been on several ships which had been torpedoed and they had been rescued time and again. The Atlantic Ocean is cruel and very cold in the winter months and some of these men had suffered from a condition called "Immersion Foot". Their feet were very swollen, with areas of numbness and pain, from being in the cold water so long before they were rescued.

It was at the Cogswell Street Military Hospital that Jack had his first encounter with a man classified as an "enemy". He was one of the German prisoners of war who had been shipped to Canada for medical treatment. To Jack, he was first a patient and then, possibly, an enemy.

■

As I was treating him, I learned that he was a German pilot who had been shot down over England. He was seriously wounded, weak, thin, and very pale. His shoulders were quite rounded from hunching over the controls of a plane for eight years. I could see he was very intelligent as he talked about the war. He said he was sure the Germans would win and all he hoped was that he could maintain his sanity until the war was over so he could return home....

One day as I was coming into the ward I heard a lot of cursing and shouting coming from the corner where the German pilot was. The Ward Sergeant was yelling at the defenceless patient and calling him a murderer who killed women and children. The German was trying to say, in broken English, that the pilots were only bombing factories and that it was an accident if any civilians were killed.

I was very angry with the Sergeant and told him he would be moved off the ward. It was a cowardly attack on his part—and from someone who had such a low-category health rating that he would never be going over to war himself. I thought it was wrong to abuse a defenceless man who was far away from home.

Jack had yet to see the human devastation wrought by the bombs dropped from German or Allied planes. He continued to treat the patients in the Cogswell Street Hospital—and he could have stayed there for the duration of the war if he had chosen to. There were doctors who preferred to stay at military hospitals in Canada. However, Jack was increasingly convinced that his training as a surgeon was desperately needed overseas.

> It became more and more apparent that the best way to serve my country was to go overseas to a combat area where my surgical training could be of some assistance to those in need. As I had just been married, this was not a pleasant thought, but it was something that Rita and I faced up to together. We knew there would be no peace in the world and no democracy as we had come to know it until the totalitarian states were defeated.

During their time at St. Michael's, the pressure of work and their involvement with each other had given them little time to really think about some of the choices they were making. Their initial decision to go to the war had been made out of a vague sense of responsibility.

Mixed in with the crush of people in Halifax, they began to realize that they were part of a worthwhile and historic struggle. Jack would go out for a beer with old friends from Saskatoon or from medical school days at McGill. Inevitably, they would talk about the course of the war, about who had gone overseas and why. Rita had time to read the papers carefully, and she grew into her own convictions.

> Our motives hadn't been that lofty when Jack joined up. The loftiness came later, in Halifax. I started to read the news. I heard about all the ships that had been sunk. I began to think about what we were giving up and why and about life in that overcrowded city where food was getting scarce. But I was glad we were part of it. I knew it was right to be part

of this. Everything we heard about the Nazis revolted us. Democracy was important, England was important to us. It was worth sacrificing something for.

In the end, they went overseas because they felt that there was something about the way of life they had known that was worth defending. They didn't know about all the evils of Nazism at that time—it was only after the war that they learned the full extent of the horrors of the concentration camps and of the atrocities the Nazis had committed elsewhere. Nevertheless, what they knew in Halifax seemed more than enough to go on. Later, when they settled down in Saskatoon after the war, Rita and Jack could never understand why people would pass up an opportunity to vote. No matter how stormy the day, they would go to the polling station to vote in whatever election was at hand—federal, provincial, municipal, or school-board. They knew what they had been willing to die for, and they knew what they wanted to live for as well.

My parents' honest description of the process through which their commitment to the war effort evolved rings true within my own experience. Perhaps there are those who emerge into life with their convictions fully formed. There may be others whose commitments are shaped by a single moment of revelation. However, most of us are drawn along by unexpected encounters and momentary insights, to the point where we cannot return without abandoning who we have become along the way. At some point, I—like my parents—came to recognize the ground on which I was already standing. It takes time to learn where one stands, upon what, and with whom. It takes moments of walking in another's shoes, dancing in the dark, standing on the corners, and stumbling along the sidestreets of life.

To take a stand means to be here and not there, with some and not others, thus and not so. Only our lives give weight to our words.

The time in Halifax was lonely and unsettling. Given the uncertainties of the war, the young couple could do little but live in the present moment.

> We didn't do much planning for the future. We had wanted to have children but it didn't seem the time or place. We had only one room so we knew we couldn't have a child. Hardly anyone had children then. There was one couple that had a little baby (they knew they would be staying in Halifax) and the rest of us all loved the baby. At that point we were just living like thousands of other people whose lives were suspended by the war. We didn't have many friends—Halifax was a navy town and we were army. But we didn't try to develop friendships either. People were just passing by and we were just passing by—putting in time before departure.

Up to that point, most of those in the Canadian army who had gone overseas were still training in England. Despite a few false starts, Canadian soldiers had seen almost no action in Europe. The dangers did not seem quite real.

■

None of us seemed to think that when we got overseas we might be sent to the front—either in North Africa or in Europe. We didn't think about being wounded or killed. The whole thing loomed more as an adventure which would have its unpleasant moments but would not last very long. We only hoped that we would be sent someplace interesting. I just wanted to get on with the job in the hope that I could get back to normal life, to Rita, and to finish my training in surgery. We didn't think too much about the grim side of the war because we didn't know about it.

In May 1942, Jack was transferred to the 4th Division and became regimental medical officer for the Governor General's Foot Guards, who were stationed at Debert, Nova Scotia. Rita moved to Truro, which was only seven miles away from the camp. Although the training sessions were long and exhausting, Jack was quite excited by what he was learning. The man who had spent hours practising with scalpels and sutures was now being taught how to operate weapons.

■

I had never had any experience with weapons and I was thrilled to get the opportunity of seeing what I could do. The Colonel was insistent that the Medical Officer take as much training as those who would be in actual fighting. We had to be able to defend ourselves and our patients, he said. I fired a Browning machine gun from a Ram tank and I also qualified in the Browning 30-yard pistol and the Tommy gun.

I drove a Bren Gun carrier truck and learned how to ride a motorcycle. It made me feel like one of the boys.

The cohesion of camp life at Debert offered Rita and Jack the opportunity of getting to know some people. They had many a good time with three officers of the Governor General's Footguards. Captain Laidlaw, their favourite, was affectionately called "Cherub" because he was short and roly-poly with a fresh pink complexion; he came from a ranching family near Medicine Hat. Captain Ted Slack, an older married man, had been raised near Ottawa. The war was a great adventure for young Lieutenant Johnny Boles, and a pleasant change from his job as a salesman with the O-Pee-Chee Gum Company. The four men would remain the best of friends—until Normandy.

Rita and the wives of several of the officers became friends in the way that wives do when their husbands share a common lot. They spent quite a bit of time together and went to parties at the camp on weekends.

We knew it wouldn't be long until our husbands left for England. Although we were worried, there was almost a festive atmosphere. At least there would be some action. The men were happier knowing they would soon be leaving. Their attitude was "Let's get over there—fight the Germans, beat them—and return and get on with our lives." I suppose we women were pleased for them.

During the whole long year of waiting, Rita and Jack had only a few days that were not scheduled according to the requirements of war. They spent them at Peggy's Cove.

It was the only holiday we had together before Jack went overseas. I suppose it was our honeymoon. It was such a beautiful place with the waves crashing upon the giant rocks. We had our own little cottage by the sea. We went boating and took long walks along the shore, realizing it could be our last time together before Jack's departure. We wanted to be able to remember those days during the times we would be apart.

Were they ever that young and in love? Yes, it seems they were. As I look at the picture of them at Peggy's Cove—the picture on the front of this book—I catch the spirit and the strength in their stance. Faces to the wind, eyes set towards the old world in Europe that they had yet to see, they looked as if there was nothing they couldn't weather together. As I look at them now, I see an older couple who can no longer stand so strong and so tall. At times, I feel the slightest breeze could blow them over. But they are still standing side by side on the shore of an unknown future.

The summer of 1942 was a low point in the war for Canadians. In their first taste of action, some 5,000 young Canadians, many of them from the prairies, were sent off on a disastrous, ill-planned raid on the French coastal town of Dieppe—a town whose flat, pebbly beaches were overlooked by a sheer wall of cliff topped by German tank and gun emplacements. Only 2,211 returned; the rest were killed or captured. At first the abortive raid was hailed as a victory, but as the reports began to roll in of the dead and the wounded there was shock across the nation. Canadians asked why such an apparently suicidal raid had been undertaken in the first place. Jack's parents in Saskatoon wrote him about the boys from the neighbourhood who had been killed at Dieppe. It was not a promising time to be thinking of going overseas.

Soon after Dieppe, Jack's unit got the call to go overseas. Before he left for Halifax, he put Rita on the train in Truro to send her back to her family in Oshawa. Each of them had thought about the possibility of Jack not returning from the war but they had not spoken to each other about it. They couldn't. It was an emotional moment for both of them.

> Our husbands took us to the train station to see us off. The day we had expected for so long had finally arrived. We had thought about it for so long and we had wondered how we would cope with it. We talked for a while with the others and then we walked farther along the platform. It was a quiet time of two people saying goodbye. There was so little to say. We thought so much.

> I tried to keep up Rita's spirit and mine too with mindless chatter. We were both in tears when I kissed her goodbye—not knowing if we would ever see each other again. I recall saying stupid things such as "with any breaks we will have this war over

in less than a year." I thought Rita's hands were cold as I finally let go of her and I suppose mine were probably the same.

V

Crossings

Jack stood waving on the platform in Truro long after the train had left. Then it was his turn to leave for Halifax and beyond.

■

> We left Debert Camp in the early morning in a torrential downpour of rain. We assembled in the Drill Hall and loaded onto open trucks for the trip down to Halifax. The trip took longer than planned because there were so many washouts on the road. When we finally arrived at the docks later in the afternoon, we were completely soaked. It was a dreary trip and I was feeling desolate.

As the train from Truro made its way north to Ontario, Rita had several days to absorb the shock of the separation and the many changes that had happened during the past year.

It was a long journey to Oshawa. I thought about the year behind us. Our life together had not gone exactly as we had hoped or planned. I thought about the year, or years, ahead for each of us. As I looked out of the window, I marvelled at the beauty of our land—and I knew it was worth fighting for.

Life is not easy for us now, I thought. But we had made a decision to fight for something worthwhile. Then I thought of all the other young couples who would be saying goodbye and of the young men who would be leaving their peacetime occupations or careers suspended.

It was a thoughtful three days' journey back to Oshawa and my parents' home. I would be one more young wife—waiting, waiting. I knew on that train that I didn't just want to put in time until the war ended.

Jack had boarded HMS *Pasteur* and on September 22, 1942 it set off for England—though not before he had posted his letters to Rita. The ship was one of eleven troopships in its convoy, with a battle cruiser and ten destroyers protecting them. It had over four thousand troops on board: Cameron Highlanders from Scotland and the West Indies, Green Howards from Yorkshire who were returning from Libya, and reinforcements for every Canadian unit overseas. There were also about a hundred Poles who were being sent to reinforce the Polish Armoured Division.

Although the *Pasteur* was a large ship, it was hardly a luxury liner.

> Fortunately, I had worked as a waiter on the Great Lakes passenger boats during the summers to put myself through medical school. It helped me deal with the pitching and rolling on HMS *Pasteur*.

Not everyone was in such good shape. The ship had picked up some infected water in Halifax so most of the men were suffering from diarrhea; Jack applied the usual remedies to help them get over their discomfort. However, there was little he could do to alleviate the irritations caused by the number of bedbugs and cockroaches on board. These were minor provocations.

The real concern was the threat from German submarines, which were wreaking considerable havoc on convoys at that time. Every morning there was an evacuation drill to prepare for the possibility of being torpedoed. If the alarms sounded, Jack was to proceed to a lifeboat with a senior naval officer and take aboard casualties, nurses, and as many others as possible.

Fortunately, the alarms never went off. The days passed slowly as the convoy made its way over the vast ocean. On September 30, Jack recorded in his diary a rather typical day on the Atlantic.

> It's cloudy today and getting colder so we know we can expect rough weather. This morning one of the ships on the starboard side was practising ack-ack firing. We could see the puffs of black smoke in the sky. We passed a school of porpoises diving in and out of the water—a much more welcome sight than

> a periscope! We black out completely around 6:30 p.m. and it is quite an experience to step on deck when it is so dark you can't see the rail and, although there are ships all around us, not a ship can be seen.

The night sky over such dark waters must have seemed all the stranger to someone accustomed to facing the darkness from firm prairie ground. As I read Dad's description of those pitch-black moments on the ocean crossing, I wonder why he, and so many others, were willing to go to a world they had only read about, to a war they knew little of, to help people whom they had never met.

Mom and Dad obviously felt some sense of responsibility for others sight unseen. Strangers entered their universe of moral concern. The older I get, the more remarkable this seems. Care and concern seem more possible with those who are friendly or familiar. Of course, those who are nearest and dearest to us may betray us, and we sometimes reject them if they are too close for comfort. Yet on the whole we tend to feel some responsibility for those who are familiar—even if that responsibility is sometimes fraught with difficulty. The familiar, at least, has a face and a name. How is it possible to have a sense of solidarity with nameless, faceless strangers—those near at hand and unknown millions throughout the world? What is it that moves us to identify with others across the distances and differences? As I read my parents' story and consider the lessons of my own life, I am beginning to see that caring for strangers is rarely a response that we can argue ourselves into or out of. Such care seems more like an act of faith, a belief in the infinite value of each human person. This is not something that can be proved or disproved. It is something that is assumed, believed in, put into practice.

The evenings on the *Pasteur* were long and Jack spent many hours playing poker with Cherub, Ted, and Johnny. Occasionally the tedium was broken by some film such as *Three Smart Girls Grow Up*, with Deanna Durbin, or *Letter of Introduction*, starring Charlie McCarthy. Sometimes the men broke out in songs from more familiar times and places. The Polish troops in particular sang with great gusto and seeming cheerfulness.

■

> However, when I had a chance to talk to some of them who could speak a little English, I could see that they were far from the happy people they seemed to be when they were singing. They told me terrible stories of what the Nazis had done in their country. Many of them had lost members of their own families and close relatives. The Poles hated the Nazis and wanted to get to England so they could be that much closer to the struggle of their own country.

Jack's original diary gives a sense of how his thoughts of Rita were woven in and out of the experiences of his day-to-day life on the ship.

■

> I miss you a lot, Beany—I have shown your picture to the two dining-room stewards already. They are two characters. One is a little English Jew by the name of Charlie Rose. He used to be the Chief Air Raid Warden of Stepney in London. He has been in

> hundreds of air raids. The other chap is a cheerful little Scot. We have lots of fun at mealtimes....
>
> The ship has stopped rolling for the moment. Went to mass in the Officer's Lounge this morning. A French Canadian sang a beautiful solo and then the Polish troops sang hymns. I have been lying in my bunk waiting for supper—just looking at your pictures in my wallet, Rita. They help a lot.

Eight days after departure, they caught sight of land. It was the coast of Ireland. As he stood on the deck of the ship, Jack was thrilled to see, even from a distance, the place where his ancestors had come from. His great-grandparents, like Rita's, had come from Ireland during the potato famine in the 1840s.

■

> It was misty but the outline of the hills became more visible as we drew closer. It seemed so welcoming—like home. We had grown up with a fierce pride in our Irish heritage and I thought back to the Sunday afternoons at our home in Saskatoon when my family would gather to listen to the records of the famous Irish tenor John McCormack.

Mom and Dad were both as Irish as Irish can be. Dad's family had come from Killaloe in County Clare and most of Mom's family had lived in County Cork. The only exceptions to this Irish Catholic stew of relatives were, on my father's side, a great-grandfather called Joseph Fischer from Bavaria, and, on my mother's side, a great-grandmother called Mary Jane Elliott, a Protestant from Armagh in the north of Ireland. Mary Jane had been married to an Anglican clergyman, but he died at sea as they were on their way to the new world. She subsequently married an Irish Catholic in Canada.

Irish as two shamrocks on the hill of Tara, and yet Rita and Jack were quite intent on doing what they could to help ·England in its hour of distress. Not all the Irish felt this way. Jack was very upset when he heard that there were German U-boats refuelling off the coast of Ireland.

For Jack and Rita it would seem that being Irish had more to do with the poetry and romance in their lives than with any political consciousness. While they had grown up hearing the songs and stories of "the troubles" associated with the British, they had also learned their history in a Canadian school. They were proud of belonging to the British Commonwealth, proud of its parliamentary tradition—and loyal. Jack saw Britain as the keeper of the democratic way of life and Rita saw it as the treasury of all the literature that had shaped her imagination from early on.

Yet being Irish also meant being Catholic. There were times when I realized that their roots ran deeper than mine in this regard. As a young adult, I bought what I thought was the most appropriate flower for a family celebration. It was an orange tiger lily, the provincial flower of Saskatchewan. My mother looked pale as I unwrapped the gift. "It's a Protestant flower," she exclaimed. Although she was active in ecumenical activities at that time, she still carried the memory of the Orange Day Parade in Ontario—the day when Protestants waved orange lilies, the day when all Catholic children were warned to stay inside.

Once past the coast of Ireland, Jack's ship docked in Scotland. From there the troops were shipped to Aldershot, where the British army had its main manning depot. For the next twenty-one months, Jack would spend his time at several hospital and medical centres in the south of England.

Soon after he arrived, Jack learned that his next-door neighbour in Saskatoon had been killed.

■

>I was in one of the local pubs and had struck up a conversation with a pilot in a Spitfire squadron. I asked him if he had run into my neighbour Cam Willis, who was a Canadian in the RAF. He looked at me and said, "Cam's gone for a Burton." I didn't understand what he meant because Burton was a brand of beer at that time. When I asked him to explain, he said, "He's dead. He was shot down in flames over France a few days ago."
>
>I was quite shaken. It was the first time that someone very close to me had been killed in the war. Cam and I had grown up together and we played golf all the time as teenagers. He had gone over to England several years before the war to train as an RAF pilot and was a very experienced flyer. I couldn't imagine our street and Saskatoon without him. I wanted to tell someone what a good golfer he was.

Jack didn't really celebrate his thirtieth birthday, which came at the end of October that year. It was not until a month later that he received his first letter from Canada. He and Rita had been writing each other every day since they had parted in Truro, but the mail across the Atlantic was slow—and not always sure. They could tell from the dates on the letters which ones were missing. Missing letters meant that a boat had gone down in the Atlantic. Missing letters meant missing people—and others who were missing them. Jack had bought a beautiful garnet cross for Rita at an antique store in Lindford and sent it to her for her birthday. She never received it.

But they kept writing.

※

> There were many things Jack couldn't write about because of wartime censorship. I wrote about my hospital work, about my relatives, about mutual friends—anything. Sometimes the letters weren't too satisfactory. There were so many questions and so few answers. I wondered about the progress of the war, about the possible invasion of Europe. He wrote about friends from Canada who turned up in England or about cases he was working on. The content of each letter didn't matter. The letters were a way of keeping in touch, a way of loving. The letters helped us hope that the war would end—that we could begin a life together.

Rita's letters told Jack that she had accepted a job as a night supervisor at Oshawa General Hospital. If she couldn't be with him, she wrote, she was at least glad to be back with her family.

Oshawa and the small towns around it were increasingly affected by the war. Many families had sons and daughters in the forces and many of those were already overseas. In the barber shops, on the assembly lines at General Motors, and in the hospital, people stopped what they were doing to listen to the radio for news of the war. They listened anxiously, for there had already been news of some hometown boys who had been killed in the war.

Nevertheless, the tide of events seemed to be shifting in favour of the Allies. The battle of El Alamein in November 1942 marked the beginning of the end of German dominance in North Africa. In January 1943 the Russian army defeated the Germans at Stalingrad. That summer the Allies would land in Sicily and begin the liberation of Europe.

The war pulled the people of Oshawa together in the same way that it was pulling the people of England together.

> After leaving the hospital in the morning I went to help out at the blood clinics, which were very busy places in those days. People were so ready to give blood. The war seemed to bring out the best in them. Older women were knitting, making dressings, and helping in many different ways. They were doing it to help the boys "over there". Everyone worked at something. Our problems and sacrifices seemed small in comparison to those of the people in Europe. There were even fewer complaints about General Motors.

The requirements of war were pushing Canada towards greater industrialization, and Rita could see rapid changes taking place around her.

> A munitions factory was set up in Ajax and the whole town was developing around the factory, which was about ten miles from our hospital. Young people from all over the country, and many women, came to work there and make munitions for the war effort. They lived in Oshawa and all the nearby towns. There were romances, weddings, and babies!

Our obstetrical unit was very busy that year. There were many babies from Ajax and often they arrived in the night when I was on duty. The Obstetrical Supervisor, Mrs. Baines, was a very experienced and wonderfully warm woman. We became good friends because of all those babies.

Some of Rita's high school friends were in the process of either getting married or having their first children. They were all working on their "hope chests". Rita never bothered getting anything for her hope chest. Her only hope was that the war would be over soon so she could begin to think about her future with Jack. In the meantime, she decided to throw all of her energy into her work at the hospital.

Oshawa General was short-staffed—short of doctors, nurses, and interns. As night supervisor, Rita had more than her share of responsibility.

When I first arrived at the hospital, I was rather concerned about how the nurses would feel having someone so young as a Night Supervisor—especially someone who had graduated from a large Toronto hospital. My predecessor had been an older woman who had her midnight meal served in her office. I decided I would rather join the grads and the students in the dining room. When I entered the dining room that first night, I heard the nurses talking about the new Night Supervisor. They asked me if I had seen her. Just then the kitchen cook came into the room. She had known me as a child and called out my name. We all laughed together.

A hospital at night has its own rhythm of life—and death. Rita enjoyed making the rounds of the floors to see the patients before they were settled in. It was a chance to chat with them— she had known some of them as a child. She would go around to see them again after midnight, walking along the dimly lit corridors. Often there was emergency surgery during the night and she and one of the younger student nurses would set up for the operations. In quieter moments, she discussed cases with some of the student nurses. These informal teaching sessions were a pleasant break in the long night.

Although Rita could not be with Jack, she sometimes shared in the closeness—and the separation—of other couples.

One remembers certain moments in a hospital which remain vivid many years later—especially if they happened during the long, dark nights. One evening an old man who had had a stroke was admitted. He was accompanied by his wife. I remembered them well because they had been friends of our family. As a child, I had thought they were a handsome couple. That night, as his charming wife and I sat in his room, I looked at them and thought that they had never seemed so beautiful as they were then in their love and concern for each other. His wife and I had tea together each night until he died. We were closer then than we had ever been before. A hospital in the middle of the night is a place like none other. Things are very clear and real.

The hospital at night was a place of love and suffering, of birth and death and all the moments in between. It was, at least once, a place of fear for Rita. A German prisoner of war from a nearby camp had been brought to the hospital for X-rays and had escaped. The police thought he might still be in the hospital.

※

> One of my responsibilities was to go over to the Annex for chronically ill patients, to see the nurse on duty and the patients. The Annex was connected to the hospital by a long, dark corridor. As I walked over to the Annex that night, I wondered what I would do if the German prisoner leaped out at me. I didn't feel very brave even with my flashlight clutched in my hand!

My mother, the timid. My mother, the brave.

By this time Jack had been in England for a year. His pictures of Rita were becoming worn with longing.

■

> Each time I looked at Rita's picture, she would look a little different. So I kept looking to make sure it was really Rita and it would make me hope that I would see her after the war—unchanged.

Then one of Jack's friends told him that his wife had been able to get over to England as a member of the British Civil Nursing Reserve. Although the Canadian army would not accept nurses who were married, the British were in desperate need of nurses in civilian hospitals to replace those who had joined the forces in Africa and elsewhere. This was all Jack needed to hear, and he wrote Rita the next day asking her to look into the possibility.

She did. Almost immediately, she received word that she should be prepared to leave for England on short notice. She resigned from Oshawa General and packed her trunk. Within days she was notified that she was to proceed to Montreal. It was just before Christmas 1943.

> I boarded the train in Oshawa. It was a long troop train filled with servicemen from all over the country. In Montreal, I met the eleven other Canadian nurses who were joining the BCNR and took another train to Halifax. Our ship was waiting for us in the harbour. It seemed very small for an ocean-going vessel.

It seemed small because it hadn't really been built for trans-Atlantic crossings in mid-winter. It had originally been used to carry bananas in the tropics, but had been commandeered into the Allied supply effort. The little banana boat would carry the twelve nurses and seventy-five RAF officers who were returning home to England after a special course in Canada. The convoy—which included many small ships but only a few supporting naval craft—left Halifax days before Christmas on a voyage which would take two weeks.

> We were told to keep warmly dressed at all times and to keep our heavy coats nearby in readiness for an emergency call to our lifeboat stations. The ship

was so cold it was easy to obey that order. We had regular exercise walking around the deck during the day. The waves were high and our little boat bobbed up and down in the cold winter sea. We watched the whole convoy and felt that the other ships and the people in them were friends. The small boats were in the centre with the larger ships and destroyers on the outside of the circle, protecting us on our way.

At night everything was so black but we could still pick out the other ships. It was eerie. The moon shone on the convoy and on the lively water. It seemed so peaceful but it was not.

One morning the nurses were told that two of the little boats had been torpedoed by U-boats who had been lurking underneath. The boats had sunk in flames in the middle of the night.

The convoy spent Christmas somewhere in the middle of the Atlantic. The news of the lost vessels made it more difficult for those on the banana boat to join their voices with the herald angels singing, "Peace on Earth, Good Will to Men".

The Christmas service in the lounge was very emotional. All of us remembered past Christmases at home with our loved ones. What a strange Christmas it was—sharing a cabin with people I hardly knew in a boat in the middle of nowhere. Would we arrive safely? Were there more German subs out there? Down there? Would Jack's unit still be in England when I arrived? If I arrived?... Our small banana boat slowly made its way through the dark water.

The passengers on board tried to make the best of their precarious lot. The nurses chatted for hours about their home towns in Canada, about their various nursing experiences, and about their husbands. Rita got to know Peggy Hutton from Calgary on that voyage. They devised elaborate schemes as to how they would contact their husbands once they were in England, and wondered about the kind of work that would await them in the civilian hospitals. Friendships formed quickly—the nurses didn't have the luxury of counting on tomorrow.

The nurses and officers also found ways to keep themselves from overdramatizing the ever-present threat of the submarines.

> The RAF men were very good at drama. They produced plays and we all took part in them. Sometimes we had amusing and original skits. We even attempted Shakespeare and spent hours learning our parts. I was Juliet in one of the plays and I remember trying to say "Romeo, Romeo, wherefore art thou Romeo?" according to the instructions of the director, a rather large man with an Oxford accent.

The little banana boat finally reached the docks of Liverpool in the middle of the night. Just as it was pulling in, the sirens began to sound. Rita and her fellow passengers had arrived at the start of a massive bombing raid on the port area.

> The city was in blackout—but it was quite bright near the docks! What welcoming fireworks! We

had read about the bombings in the newspapers but this was the real thing. It took quite some time to get everyone off the ship. I sat on my trunk near the dock waiting to see what would happen next. Strangely enough, I felt quite calm. It was so good to be on land. I felt somewhat detached from what was going on around me. There was lots of yelling and shouting. I heard the Liverpool accent for the first time and watched all the hustle and bustle. What a cheerful lot those dock workers were! At last we were in England and we were prepared to do whatever was asked of us to help in the war effort. I was glad, sitting there on my trunk, that I had come to England to do my bit. I felt my life in Canada had been a little too comfortable.

As soon as some transportation could be found, the nurses were taken in a truck to a large hospital, where they were given food and some strong tea. They were even allowed a bath.

A real bath in a tub. What a luxury! We hadn't had a tub bath since leaving Canada. The tub in the bathroom had a black painted line around it only a few inches from the bottom. We were told that we were allowed water only to that black line. We were so grateful to have a bath that we would have taken one in an inch of water.

That night we found ways to phone our husbands, all of whom were stationed in southern England. Jack had been expecting me but he didn't know when I would be arriving. It had been a long journey. We had been separated since September 1942. It was now January 1944. Would Jack be as happy to see me as I would be to see him? I dialed to reach him at Dorking in Surrey.

The phone call came through to Jack while he was sitting in the mess where he was stationed in Dorking. He was told it was a "trunk call", or a long distance call.

■

A voice came over the line saying, "Hello...hello! How are you, big boy?" I asked, "Who is that speaking?" I didn't recognize the voice as there was a great deal of noise on the line. Then the voice said, "This is Rita. I have just landed in Liverpool and all that noise is because there is a big bombing raid on." Then she added, "You didn't tell me it would be like this!" I laughed and said, "I didn't tell you because when I wrote you I wasn't sure that there would be a big raid on the night you landed!" We laughed together and of course I was thrilled. We arranged to meet the next day in London.

In spite of all the phone lines which had been damaged in Liverpool and elsewhere throughout England, the nurses found ways to get in touch with their husbands. All twelve husbands were there to greet them when the train pulled into Victoria Station. It had been a year and a half since Jack had put her onto one train; now he was lifting her off another. Rita was ecstatic.

We were in London! We were together! We stayed at the Dominion Hotel at Lancaster Gate. It was a small hotel and most of the guests were elderly. The first morning as we were going down the stairs for breakfast, we passed several dear old ladies on their way into the dining room. One of them turned and said to me, "Just over from Canada, are you, dear?" I told her that I had just arrived in the middle of a raid. "You'll get used to it after a while, dear," she said, "it's not as bad as it was in the blitz."

We spent the next two days walking around London. Jack had been there a few times on leave but it was all new to me and I was fascinated. This beautiful old city was very shabby and dirty and crowded with service people on leave. There were large craters where buildings must have been. There was lots of rubble and sandbags everywhere. The people on the street were cheerful but their faces showed the strain of living in war-torn London—the bombing raids, the food shortages and family worries. Jack told me that many had been bombed out of their homes and many children had been sent out of the city for safety.

One day we walked along the Strand and into Fleet Street. It was wonderful to see St. Paul's and all the places I had only read about.

We had dinner at a fine restaurant one night—pigeon pie, considered a great treat, was on the menu. We went to see a play, *Blithe Spirit*, and during the play there was an air raid. Noel Coward came on stage and said the play would be stopped for a short time to allow people to leave for the shelters if they wished. He said, "The show will go on." We decided to stay.

VI

Neither Here nor There

The south of England had become a large holding area for the Allied troops who were being assembled for the eventual invasion of Europe. Some of the Canadian troops were there for years before they saw any action. They were in an in-between time in an in-between place. They were neither here nor there—no longer in Canada but not yet in the thick of the fighting. For some, the delay was a marvellous opportunity to pursue the possibility of marriage with one of the girls in the nearby villages. For many, it was simply a time of infuriating boredom and frustration.

■

Most of the men had been away from home for quite some time. During their days off, they would go up to London or another centre to see if they could get some decent food or drink. This could be quite a challenge because the pub owners kept the liquor for their regular customers and would only sell beer to the soldiers.

The men would get into arguments or fights over nothing. There were those who got involved with women whose husbands were in the Far East or the Middle East. Then they would get into difficulties not only with the women but with the women's relatives as well. Other men would pick up some of the street girls in London and we soon had to treat quite a few cases of VD.

There were men who simply didn't return after their leave, and they would be listed AWOL. If this happened too often, they would end up in a military prison for 28 days. They were forced to sleep on the floor on blankets and they had to get up at the crack of dawn. The boys who came back from this sort of discipline usually didn't want to go back again.

The boisterous young Canadians were not always popular in the small villages in the south of England. Some of them had never had a drink at home, and didn't know how to handle the beer which was a normal part of life in the local pubs. But Jack would later reflect that those who did endure the time of waiting were not automatically prepared for action when the time came.

■

The men who had difficulty sticking to the rigid discipline during the months of waiting were often great in action and others who seemed so steady did not measure up when things got hotter. Some of the officers who seemed first class proved to be indecisive in battle while others, particularly junior officers, turned out to be real leaders when they got away from the boredom of everyday camp life.

So much in life, as in war, seems to be in the waiting. Dad spent twice as much time preparing to go to war as he ever spent in the field of action. But it depends on how one waits and why. As I think over my own life, I see how much of it has been preparatory for the few moments of decision, of acting and speaking, that made some difference. All I had to go on in those moments was whoever I had become by that point. There was never enough time to think, rarely enough time to weigh all the consequences. There was only whatever remained in the mind of my heart from long hours of study and solitude, from all the delightfully useless interludes with friends, from the many encounters with realities too wonderful or too harsh to ignore. It is good to wait on life. It is also important to know that there are times when life calls for and awaits our response.

Jack was just as bored as everyone else, especially during the year and a half before Rita came. There was lots, however, that had to be done before the long-awaited invasion of France. Although he had gone to England as the medical officer for the Governor General's Foot Guards, he was transferred within a year to a casualty clearing station where his surgical skills would be used more fully. It was one of three casualty clearing stations being prepared to accompany the Canadian troops into Normandy.

The station itself bore some resemblance to the M.A.S.H. unit in the television series of the seventies. This was one of my favourite shows. Dad never enjoyed watching it because it was "too Hollywood", but he would refer to it to explain the kind of station they had put together in England.

The main challenge for those working in the casualty clearing station was to supply immediate treatment for those too seriously wounded to be transported directly back to a base hospital in England. There were about fifty people in Casualty Clearing Station #6, including nine officers (two of whom were in charge of surgical operating teams), three padres, about eight nurses, and a dentist, adjutant, and quartermaster. The support staff consisted of cooks, orderlies, radio operators, and so on. The facilities planned included a series of tents: a resuscitation tent where the wounded would be taken on arrival and stabilized to the point where they could withstand surgery; a large tent which would become the operating room; a number of other tents for post-operative care; a mess tent for eating and socializing; and several small tents for sleeping quarters.

Jack used the long months to prepare himself for the surgery, which he knew would have to be done under great pressure. He attended courses on resuscitation and transfusion and took voluminous notes on how to deal with patients in shock. He worked on designing a way for the station to refrigerate and store blood and plasma and drew a plan for setting up a resuscitation unit. Penicillin was being used for the first time; he tried to get some understanding of how it worked and what dosages were most appropriate. He went to see the famous surgeon Mr. Rodney Maingot operate, and then to Oxford to learn from the innovative Spanish surgeon Trueta, who had had a great deal of experience during the Spanish Civil War.

■

We were all rather jaded and tired because of the repetitious work, which was not very stimulating, medically speaking. I tried to attend some of the many courses in surgery which were to be found in the large centres around England and Scotland. The teachers were excellent, often older men who were unable to serve in the forces—although it was remarkable how many of them had served in the early fighting in France or even in North Africa and were now back teaching.

I attended rounds at the Royal Infirmary in Edinburgh conducted by Sir John Frazer, a brilliant man. I would sit in on some of his classes in the large amphitheatre where he taught. He would point his bony finger up into seats and say, "Would you come down here, Canada, please." One of us would go down to examine a patient with a large thyroid or a particular swelling in the abdomen. This kind of experience always stimulated us mentally and we would go back to our chores more or less cheerfully.

From time to time the station would participate in an exercise with the rest of the Canadian forces. These exercises were intended to simulate some of the battle conditions which the troops would encounter in Europe. The units would be sent hopping across the countryside at breakneck speed for two weeks. For those who were with the casualty clearing station, it meant first setting up the tents and equipment and then tearing them down, loading them on trucks, and proceeding to the next destination. It was a gruelling exercise but only the slightest preparation for the pace of action in Normandy.

When he was not working medically or out on some exercise, Jack would join in the sports teams. He had always loved sports when he was growing up, and there was ample opportunity for them in England. He played soccer and volleyball, and learned to pitch horseshoes and to play billiards, snooker, and poker with the best of them.

Through his involvement in games that included some of the local men, and during the times when he went to London to replace civilian doctors, Jack developed a deep respect for the English people.

■

> They looked very tired but somehow they managed to keep very cheerful in spite of the loss of many of their friends and relatives. I think they were able to do so because of their gift for understatement and their ability to discuss trivia. Whenever something particularly grim had happened in a part of London or someplace else following a bombing, it was always, "Well, we must carry on—would you like a cup of tea?" The wounded British boys seemed to be much more patient and stoical than the Canadian boys.

However, Jack was less respectful of some other British attitudes.

■

> During the "Spartan Exercise", both officers and men had to line up together for each meal instead of having separate messes. This upset some of the British officers who were definitely snobs and did not like eating with the men. The Canadian officers got a kick out of this and would take great glee in telling a British officer to get into the line with the rest of us and wait his turn.

During the months before Rita came, Jack whiled away many an hour chewing the fat about nothing and everything. At the time he found some of the conversations interesting. Later, he would find them more than perceptive.

I had an interesting conversation with Lieutenant-Colonel Tweedsmuir, who was in command of a regiment which was to go to Italy. We got to talking about the Russians. I thought it was great that they were starting to control the fighting on the Eastern Front and said that we were certainly lucky to have them on our side. Tweedsmuir said, "That may be, but remember that they were on Hitler's side briefly, and after the war they will be a great threat to world peace because the Communists are dedicated to world domination." He was the only officer I met during those days who ever brought up that question....

At one point I relieved the medical officer of the 4th Medium Artillery Regiment RCA. This was a French-speaking regiment and I felt a little lonely in it. However, I was able to converse with a few of them in my high-school French or in their English. One evening two of the young lieutenants talked to me about what could happen in Quebec after the war.... They raised the possibility of Separatism. I didn't have the foggiest idea what they were talking about. They made it very clear to me that they considered me a "foreigner" because I could not speak French very well and I was not born in Quebec. They were sure that there would be an attempt made by French-speaking Quebec citizens to insist on more control of their economy and government. I was shocked when they said they would use any method, short of an armed revolution, to wrest power from the English-speaking minority.

It appears that there were some who were thinking about life after the war even before the war had really begun for them.

Once Rita arrived in England, Jack was more inclined to focus on the present. He was still waiting but now it was different. He was waiting with someone. There is a gap in his diary from January 1944 until he left for Normandy in July of that year. It seems that the only time he ever wrote in his diary was when Rita was not there to take away the phantoms of the night.

In the spring of 1944, it was apparent to all that something was beginning to develop. There was an excitement in the air. There was movement on the roads as American, British, and Canadian vehicles made their way from one point to another. Jack ran into a young Canadian journalist by the name of Charles Lynch who asserted that his presence on the scene meant something important was about to happen!

For Rita and Jack it was simply spring. At that point they were living only a few miles from each other. Rita had been stationed at the hospital in Leatherhead, which was near Dorking.

> Jack and I acquired two old bikes. We cycled back and forth between Leatherhead and Dorking. Spring was so beautiful that year. The countryside of Surrey was filled with colour—the lovely old trees and the masses of flowers. Of course there were signs of war but there were also signs of spring. I had always loved Robert Browning's poem "Oh, to be in England/ Now that April's there." I said to Jack, "We are here and it is April. How wonderful—war or not!"

They had several favourite spots that glorious spring. They preferred staying in the countryside of Surrey even over going into London. There was a lovely hotel at Box Hill, midway between Leatherhead and Dorking, where they often stopped for tea. Rita thought it was a terribly romantic place because Lord Nelson and his mistress, Lady Hamilton, had stayed there. Another special spot was a small hotel called "The Bull" in Leatherhead, when they would have gin and orange in the garden before another elegant meal of pigeon pie, and return to the garden for coffee.

They loved exploring the country lanes and the quaint little villages of Surrey together. Every hour was precious. The day of the invasion was drawing closer. And both Rita and Jack knew that, because of security, he would not be able to warn her of when he was going to leave, or even to say goodbye.

Most of Rita's time was spent in the hospital in Leatherhead. She who had imagined the places described by Galsworthy, Thomas Hardy, and the Brontës had a certain initial disappointment at being sent to a place with such a name.

> I had hoped to be sent to a little English village with a very English-sounding name. Leatherhead sounded like a place in western Canada!

However, she quickly adjusted both to the name and to the realities of life in England. She got her ration book and her monthly supply of margarine, jam, and cheese along with everyone else. She even got used to taking her helmet with her wherever she went—in case of air raids.

The building had been a school for the blind before the war but was now being used for victims of the bombing raids on London. The staff and patients had been sent down from Guy's Hospital in London. It was felt that Leatherhead would be a safer place for surgery.

The patients would arrive with no belongings after their homes had been hit. They worried more about their lost dentures and glasses than about the other possessions they had lost. Put into huge wards, in small narrow beds with thin mattresses, they never complained. They were usually from the east end of London or the suburbs in the south of London. Class distinctions seemed so unimportant in the great upheaval we were all trying to live through.

However, the British nurses insisted on drawing some distinctions among the staff, and Rita found this difficult to adjust to. Although the Canadian nurses were far more qualified than most of the British nurses there, Rita noticed that she and her compatriots were being "put down".

The matron told us that the Canadian nurses would be called staff duty nurses [floor duty nurses] no matter what our experience or qualifications had been in Canada. I was called "staff" all the time I was on duty. I rarely heard my own name spoken. The supervisors were all called "sister". I soon realized that they felt a little insecure with us—we were a little better dressed because they couldn't get clothes in England. Our training had been much different from theirs—which was based on an apprenticeship system and took longer.

However, Rita put up with the daily tension between the British and Canadian nurses. She knew she was doing what she could in the war effort and she was able to be close to Jack. When he was away on a course or an assignment, she would sit under a tree and read. Although the Leatherhead library was no more than a small collection of books in the Boots Pharmacy, she had joined it at the first opportunity.

It was not always easy to get a quiet corner to read in. Leatherhead was close enough to London that German planes would sometimes unload their extra bombs there after they had finished a raid. However, the people down below had some warning when they heard the sound of the planes passing overhead, and could take cover.

As the invasion date grew nearer, changes took place in the hospital at Leatherhead. Extra beds were installed in the men's ward. Rita was transferred to the operating room, which was being organized to receive more cases. It had only the most essential equipment—four operating tables, with no drapes between them and no sheets to put under or over the patients. The instruments were boiled, sterilized in a primitive way, on a gas burner between cases.

Jack began to receive instructions that were clearly different in tone. The doctors were told that, since the German surgeons had operated on wounded Allied soldiers and helped to save them, they would be expected to do the same for the German wounded. The instructions were to treat Allied troops first provided that there was good reason—*i.e.*, provided that their wounds were more serious. Then they were to operate on the Germans.

The members of the station were also instructed by a young British officer who had escaped from the Germans, on what to do if they were captured in France.

■

> The first point he impressed upon us was that our best chance to escape was immediately after capture, while being taken to the rear. If one could do this, then French civilians would not be involved. He said that he had made the mistake of killing one of his German captors at the time he was being sheltered by French resistance fighters in a town. As a result, French civilians were taken as hostages and shot.
>
> He went on to say what one should do if one escaped. After hiding at night, one should then be on the lookout for a peasant standing in the centre of a field. If one was sure that there were no Germans around, one was to go out and just stand there until spoken to. The man in the field was a "pilot" who would take you to a house. When the time was right, another man or woman would act as a courier and take you to another courier who would turn you over to a "passer". This system of passers and couriers would eventually take you to the south of France and over the Spanish border. A good many Allied airmen who had been shot down had escaped along this route.

These arrangements were a small part of the massive preparations which had been made for the Allied invasion of Europe. It all came down to one day—D-Day, planned for June 5, 1944, but postponed to June 6 because of unfavourable weather. Jack had expected to be leaving on D plus 5 but the departure was delayed because of more bad weather. It was Rita, rather than Jack, who was immediately caught up in the aftermath of D-Day. The first casualties were flown back across the Channel and sent by train, ambulance, and truck to hospitals such as Leatherhead. At the end of the day, Rita phoned Jack at Dorking.

> Fortunately Rita was able to get through to me. She had no way of knowing whether I was part of the landing or not. She said to me that "the fact I got through to you on the phone tells me that you haven't gone yet but I am sure you will be gone before too long." Then she teased me, saying, "Would you like to see a war casualty, big boy?" All I could say was, "Damn!" I had been writing her every day when she was in Canada, telling her how hard things were, how bad the food was. And here it was she who had been living on civilian rations, which were far worse than ours. And then on D-day it was her hospital which was flooded with casualties. When she phoned she had been working all day long in the operating room.

Jack cycled over to Leatherhead the next day to see Rita and the patients. His unit was ready to go at any moment but he did not know when. The sight of the disfigured young men was as sobering for him as it was for Rita and the entire hospital staff. All the nurses, British and Canadian, pulled together to do what they could for the newly arrived casualties.

We nurses worked as long as was necessary in the operating room to look after the young men who were being brought back from France. Sometimes 60 patients were driven in at once. Four of them were operated on at a time. We didn't feel tired. We just kept going. After looking after a convoy of the wounded, we would go back to the nurses' residence to rest for a while. A little maid brought us hot, strong tea. For some reason, I remember her very well. She was from Twickenham. When the next convoy of wounded arrived, we were called back to the operating room and remained there until they were all looked after. My heart ached for some of these young men. Some of them woke to find out that they had been paralysed from the waist down. They would never fully recover from the war. Their bodies would carry the memory of landing on the beaches of Normandy.

Shortly after D-Day, the V-1 bombs (or buzz bombs) started falling. The precursors of modern guided missiles, the V-1s were aimed at London but often fell short of their target on places such as Leatherhead. The bombs made a putt-putt sound which would cut out just before they fell and exploded. It was very little warning. For the people of England, who had already been through so much, this latest in weaponry was upsetting and demoralizing. Rita and the other nurses in her dormitory got used to sleeping under their beds with the blankets overhanging the sides to the floor, and their helmets nearby; they worried that the dormitory windows would be blown in, sending a spray of shattered glass across the room.

We knew we were safe as long as we could hear the sound of the motor. One day we were in the dining room, a large hall with rows of long, white tables, and we heard a loud explosion nearby. The windows of the dining room were open. When we started to eat our dessert we noticed little specks of earth in our semolina pudding. We laughed and said, "Raisins in our semolina!" We had to laugh because those rockets really unnerved us.

One day Rita and Jack managed to get enough time to go for a walk in the country. As they were standing underneath a lovely old tree, they heard the motor of a buzz bomb cut out. Jack threw Rita to the ground and tried to cover her. When they got up after the explosion, they looked up and saw that all the leaves of the tree were in shreds.

It would be their last walk together for some time. On July 4, Jack's unit received notice that it would be moving out for Normandy. Contacting Rita was out of the question.

There was no way of letting Rita know that our unit was to move out from Dorking at 2:40 in the morning of July 5. After we left Dorking we stopped at the crossroads at Leatherhead. I looked up at the second-floor window of the hospital. It was Rita's room. There were no lights on. It was the middle of the night. She would have no way of knowing I was down below and on my way to France. Will I ever see you again? After a short pause to clear traffic, our convoy slowly moved on.

I wondered why Jack hadn't phoned. We had arranged to meet that night for dinner if things were quiet at the hospital. I wondered if his unit was preparing to leave.

During the night of July 5, we were called to the operating room as more casualties had arrived. In the morning, people at the hospital seemed to know that the Canadians had gone that night. The operating room staff were so kind to me when they learned my husband had gone to France. One intern, whom I had not liked very much, gave me an egg. I hadn't had an egg in months and I knew he gave me the egg as a way of saying he was sorry I was now alone in England.

VII

"The Sickly Sweet Smell of Death"

Jack's convoy rolled past the crossroads at Leatherhead and began heading north to London. They boarded their ships at the Tilbury docks, which were under fire from V-1 rockets. Two nights later they sailed down the Thames River and headed for the Straits of Dover.

■

We were told that almost every convoy had lost some ships while going through the Straits of Dover. There were big German guns at Calais which were able to fire across the Channel at this narrow point. The passengers were all ordered to roll out their hammocks and not to come up on deck in order to allow the crew greater freedom of movement in case of an emergency. The three surgeons of the casualty clearing station, Joe Luke, Bill Bigelow, and myself, lay on our hammocks below, smoking one cigarette after another—particularly as we went through the Straits just after midnight. Our conversation was light and pointless. My palms felt sweaty.

The convoy made it through the Straits and moved across the Channel, finally landing at Graye-sur-Mer, the same place where the Winnipeg Rifles had landed on D-day. As they walked off the boats and onto the beach, Jack remarked to Bill Bigelow that it wasn't like in the newsreels of D-day, when the men had jumped off the boats and into water up to their waists. "We're supposed to get into this war up to our waists, Bill."

But Jack and Bill Bigelow were up to their waists soon enough, digging out a place to sleep. Each needed a space large enough for a cot, three feet below ground; it was the only safe place to sleep because the German planes were strafing the tents. By July 13, they had set up a casualty clearing station four miles north of Caen at a little village called Cazelle. Although the invasion of Normandy had taken place a month before, the Allied troops had made very little headway and were still fighting around the town of Caen. The Germans were putting up a stiff resistance with their highly trained troops and disciplined Panzer (tank) divisions. Canadian units had had the task of trying to capture Carpiquet airport, just outside of Caen.

The casualties started to pour in to the station. The wounded were first picked up in the fields around Caen by stretcher bearers, who took them to the closest field unit; there, medics did what they could to stop the bleeding. The most serious and urgent cases were sent by truck or ambulance back to the casualty clearing station. Once they arrived, the wounded were taken to the resuscitation tent, where staff tried to get their blood pressure to the point where they could tolerate surgery. Speed was of the essence. It had all come down to this. After years of training, after months of preparation, the surgeons could only use whatever skills time would allow to save those whose lives hung in the balance.

For two weeks straight, Jack worked in the resuscitation unit—initially for shifts of eight hours on and eight hours off, but then, when this proved to be too exhausting, for shifts of twelve hours on and twelve hours off. One of his biggest concerns was the number of men whose loss of blood had put them in a state of "irreversible shock". Their blood pressure had dropped so low that no amount of replacement blood or plasma could seem to bring it up again. Many of them never made it to the operating tent.

There were days when over a hundred men passed through the resuscitation unit, a number of them badly mangled. The size of the bombs that had been developed in the Second World War, the effectiveness of the shells and mortars, had left so many men literally in pieces. Jack just kept working. He didn't have time to think. Only once did he stop to reflect on what was happening around him, and then he scribbled in his diary:

■

> It has just occurred to me. We have been shelled! bombed! machine gunned! Mines all around me! Some war!

The only other thing he noted with some interest was a hot-water shower which had been captured from the Germans and promptly installed at the station.

At the beginning of August 1944, the unit shut down for a few days to allow everyone a chance to recuperate. Jack went into Caen to see the town, which had been heavily bombed by the Allies. It was almost completely in ruins. On the way back he met Captain Gordon Young, whom he had known as a student at McGill.

■

> Gordon looked pretty shaken up at the time. He was very tired and sat down. He told me about some of his experiences as a medical officer on D-Day and after. He said that his medical training had prepared him to deal with the wounded and with death. But he was shattered one day when the ammunition vehicle one of his friends was driving was hit by enemy fire and blew up. Gordon was not far away and ran towards the wreckage. He stopped short when he saw something lying on the road. He realized that it was the liver of his friend. Gordon started to vomit. He said that it was the one thing that he could not get out of his mind.

They all saw things they could not forget and yet had to forget. A major in the Canadian army turned pale as he told Jack about seeing three French collaborators forced to dig their graves in a nearby field. They were then strapped to posts and shot by members of the resistance.

Jack remembered some of the children he had seen around Caen.

■

> I was walking through a nearby village that had been badly shelled. As I passed a small house, I noticed the window had been blown out. Then I heard the sound of children laughing. As I looked in, I saw a small boy and girl about three and four years of age. Their faces were dirty and their clothes were

in rags. They were barefoot. Each had a knife and fork and they were banging on the table. However, there was no food to be seen and there were no adults around. Perhaps they had been killed or they were off looking for food. I almost started to cry. What did these children know about the war? What did they have to do with it?

One day an ambulance drove up to our reception tent. The driver got out and asked me to take a look at a couple of casualties. He said, "I don't think you can help them but take a look anyway." I was shocked to see two little French boys about eight years old. Their bodies were shattered almost beyond recognition. Obviously, they had walked into a minefield or been hit by a shell. They were quite dead. They had on the remains of little black berets and short dark pants. I did cry then. It was all so wrong.

The short break from the pressured work at the casualty clearing station had given Jack a little time to feel something of the horror he was living through. One night, he and Captain Clare Evans got a bottle of rather green Calvados.

■

Clare and I wandered down the road beyond the station singing away. Eventually, we stumbled off the road and into a wheatfield. Suddenly I looked down and saw the German word *"Minen"*. Clare was just in front of me, weaving along. I grabbed him and persuaded him to stop so we could try and retrace our steps back onto the road. I moved slowly and kept my hand on his shoulder as we walked on the beaten-down wheat.

It was cold and foggy as we stumbled back to the camp. I said to Clare, "This is a rather dangerous place to be—why don't we get the hell out of here and go back to England?" He made a wise observation given his condition. "I think you have a good idea but unless you are a good swimmer, you will never make it across the Channel." After more drunken curses, we agreed that there was nothing for us but to go to bed. Unfortunately, we ended up outside the nurses' tents, singing away to the annoyance of all concerned. Finally, Major Jaimet came out of his tent across the way and told us to stop our vulgar singing and to go to bed at once. We agreed that this was sensible and saluted him somewhat sloppily.

In truth there was no escaping the reality of war, and the next day Jack was back at the casualty clearing station receiving a number of wounded Germans. He was committed to treating them as patients rather than as enemies.

■

Most of them were young men who were unconscious when they came in. I felt that they were just taking orders from someone else who was older. We tried to treat them with compassion because it could have been one of us. When they began to get a little better, they tried to talk with the nurses and doctors and we would talk to them a little. We were curious as to where they were from and what made them tick. I thought that I might even like some of them in another situation.

But I didn't like those who had been in the Hitler Youth Movement at all. They were totally brainwashed. At first they would throw temper tantrums and sulk. It was quite a shock for them to find out that they were not members of the "master race" as they had been taught but just like everybody else. In this war, they were just wounded men like the others. They soon lost their arrogance and had crying and hysterical spells.

Not only did Jack find himself working to save the lives of those who were the enemy. He also found himself struggling to save Canadian and British boys who had been wounded not by the Germans but by Allied bombers. The fighting was close and mistakes of great human consequence were made. The young boys in the Allied army would be waving to their planes as they flew over to bomb the Germans—only to watch in horror as the bay doors opened and bombs began to fall on them.

The battlelines on the ground are never drawn as neatly as they are on the maps used in strategy sessions. In the confusion of the moment, there is often as much to fear from allies as from enemies. The men in the bombers never had to face the real impact of their mistakes. That was left to those below.

■

It was a hot summer day and some of the officers and men had gone to swim at a beach at a place called Luc-sur-Mer. I was in the rear party when a dispatch rider in a motorcycle roared up to me and told us that there were many casualties on the way. Apparently our bombers had bombed some of our own troops. We raced back to the station. That day 221 wounded men passed through our receiving tent. We were able to save some but not all.

Jack struggled to keep a certain professional distance which would allow him to function in the midst of all of this. It usually worked, but not always.

■

I was in the resuscitation unit when they brought in Sergeant Tubbe, who was from my old regiment, the Governor General's Foot Guards. He was lying on a stretcher and looking badly shaken and dazed. When I had got him somewhat stabilized, I asked him for news of my friends Cherub Laidlaw, Johnny Boles, and Ted Slack. I started to reel when he told me they had all just been killed. Their unit, he mumbled, had lost its way and had been slaughtered by 88mm guns shooting at them from high ground. Many men had been lost trying to fight off the German tanks. It was their first action.

I was shaken by this news but I couldn't dwell on it. There was so much death and destruction all around. There were so many dying men we had to look after. Still I was shocked. I shouldn't have been because we saw the casualties of war all the time. I was so busy that I was numb to the sight of the dying and the dead. Even the news of Cherub and the others was temporarily forgotten.

There was only one place where Jack could risk remembering what he had seen and felt. The village of Cazelle was just down the road, and the little church was one of the few buildings that had been left standing after a massive bombardment. Sunday services were held there—the Catholic and Protestant services scheduled at different times. Many of the men went to the services but weren't too concerned which one they attended. Jack would go down to the church for a few minutes when he was not on duty. It became his place of refuge.

■

> I would think about Rita, about Cherub and Ted and Johnny and the French children. I would reflect on my chances of getting killed, of not going home. I prayed to God that I could live, that the war could be over. It was quiet. Sometimes I started to hear the screams of the wounded men echoing in the church. Then it was quiet again. Sometimes I just sat there—breathing.

The church of Cazelle (the town has now been renamed Mathieu) was one of the places that Dad insisted we see when my mother, sister, and I accompanied him on a trip back to Normandy in the summer of 1985. He had often spoken of this church at home, and of how important it had been to him. We felt we were going to a place of pilgrimage.

When we reached the church Dad was delighted and wanted to go inside right away. The rest of us were reduced to silence until my mother finally said what my sister and I were already thinking: "My God, it's ugly."

Ugly was the word. The walls were beige stones stained and covered with fungus. On the roof was something that looked more like a chimney than a bell tower. In any case, there was no bell to ring. Not a single flower or blade of grass grew in the grim clay ground around.

The churchyard was also the graveyard—so crowded with tombs that the gravestones had become the front steps of the church. We remarked that it was like a scene from a Gothic horror movie. Dad looked at us rather blankly. In 1944, he had never really noticed what the church looked like. "It looked pretty good at the time," he said. "It was a place to go and pray." We teased him about his spiritual home.

I later realized that we had spoken the truth, albeit flippantly. This was where he was at home in the world, where he knew who he was with God. He was far more at home there than in all the nice churches he would attend on Sundays in his later life. He was far more at home in those real talks with God than in all the trendy discussions about the church in the modern world in later years. Somewhere, sometime—I don't know where or when, but perhaps in this church—he came to his own home truths.

Cherub, Ted, and Johnny are buried in the Canadian cemetery at Bretteville-sur-Laize. This was another place of pilgrimage on our trip to Normandy that summer. Silence reigned supreme over the row upon row of white headstones— an army of witnesses who would never be able to testify about the tragedy of war.

The cemetery was so ordered and organized that we were able to find the graves of Dad's friends quite easily. We soon noticed that, even in death, they were among the more fortunate. At least death had not robbed them of their names, which were chiselled in the stone. Other headstones indicated only that "A Canadian Soldier" was buried beneath—unidentified parts that could no longer be made whole, pieces of humanity that could not be gathered under a name.

In the middle of August 1944, the casualty clearing station was moved to Hautmesnil, a place ten miles south of Caen on the road to Falaise. A visitor to Hautmesnil today would see only quiet fields with contented cows chewing away. During the war, though, this was the scene of some of the most vicious fighting in Normandy. The British and Canadians were pushing south and the Americans were fighting their way north in an attempt to meet each other at Falaise and so cut off the possibility of the First German Army escaping to the east. This was the attempt to close the "Falaise Gap". Inexplicably, the American army was ordered to stop short at Argentan and it was left to the British and Canadians to try to close the gap. The Germans fought desperately to get out. They suffered severe losses but managed to escape with half of the army intact. Historians have tried to locate the responsibility for the fateful decision to hold the Americans at Argentan. Wherever that responsibility lies, the decision had serious consequences for the Canadians, who were seeing their first fighting against a highly trained and desperate German army. Some would argue that the failure to close the gap at Falaise quickly prolonged the war for months.

The fiercest fighting took place around Trun, which became known as the "killing fields". Many of the Polish soldiers whom Jack had met on the voyage to England were killed here. In his diary Jack noted briefly, "Men dying like flies." The smell of death hung over the fields.

■

> The day we moved to Hautmesnil we set up the tents of our unit in an open field which was on the edge of a huge bomb crater. As we were setting up our tent, I noticed a familiar odour which has often been described as "the sickly sweet smell of death". We searched around for a body and finally found one, covered with large black flies, in the hedgerows not far from us. It was the body of

> a soldier of the 12th Field Artillery Canadian Regiment. I remember clearly the name on his dogtag. He had obviously been killed by one of the bombs which had been dropped by our own planes. We immediately dug a grave for this unfortunate soldier.

Within the casualty clearing station, the men had different ways of coping with the carnage all about them. Some spent more time complaining about the food in the mess than about the Germans. Others told the same jokes over and over and others went on talking morning, noon, and night.

■

> Charlie Jaimet, our medical man, just kept talking. He had sworn he would get to stay in a base hospital when we were in England but he went to Normandy. He just kept talking there, doing a fine job but telling us we were all fools and as soon as he could he was going back to England. But he kept on working and talking. That's how he coped.

There were those who found comfort in someone else's arms. In Normandy, as elsewhere, men and women reached out for someone near at hand to take away the terror of the night. Many were younger people who had no surety that there would be a tomorrow, so they lived for the day and for each other. Jack didn't understand this but he refused to pass judgement.

■

> We were all living under enormous pressure—not knowing whether we would see tomorrow or our wives or husbands again. It was tough for everyone—including those we had left behind. I didn't see any point in making it worse by being unfaithful. Each of us handled the stress in his own way but we all poured ourselves into our work.

Not everyone coped. There were young Canadian boys who cracked under the strain.

■

> Some of them had seen their buddies blown to smithereens. They would be picked up wandering around on a road or huddled by some tree. They were brought into the station, where we had set up a special ward for them. They would be crying hysterically or just sitting and staring into space. There were those who trembled and shook uncontrollably. They were in shock but with no visible wounds. The doctor in charge of them would give them sedatives and get them to sleep. When the worst was over they were shipped back to a hospital in England.

What can be said about the fear that gripped these boys? How can we judge a fear which is neither a source of courage nor a basis for cowardice? What would have been a "normal" response to such an abnormal situation? The rules and values upon which ordinary life was based had become twisted by the ruthless logic of war.

The line between innocence and guilt, which is only finely drawn in more peaceful situations, is inevitably blurred in times of war. War in itself is such a moral compromise that those who become involved in it, for whatever reason, are themselves inevitably compromised by it. However moral the decision to enter a war may be, once a person is involved in it, the whole sense of morality begins to disintegrate.

Many experienced this moral disintegration during the Second World War. Their experience is not a commentary on their personal weakness but rather a statement about the overwhelming and perverted reality of war: the bomber pilot who knew that many civilians in the vicinity of a military target would be killed; the resistance fighters who faced the fact that their actions would bring reprisals against innocent people; the bystander whose very silence became complicity; the Jewish man at Auschwitz who was forced by his captors to make a choice between sending his father or his son to the gas chamber. No one comes out of war feeling clean.

Jack's experiences of the insoluble moral dilemmas of war were not as dramatic but they were just as real. One of the moral inversions of this war—and others—was that the good came out of it feeling guilty for not having done enough, for not always having done the perfect thing, while those who had committed great crimes felt they had done nothing wrong at all.

As a doctor and an officer, Jack was forced to make choices between two options—neither of which seemed right.

We had been given instructions that we were to give priority to Canadians and British and Poles over Germans—within reason. The decisions were difficult but we had to be firm. Usually, it was very clear

> which patient was most in need of urgent attention. But sometimes there were so many patients that we didn't have time to weigh all the considerations....
>
> The French villagers suffered a great deal. One day Padre Papineau came to my tent and asked me if I, as officer-in-charge, would authorize sending our water wagon to the village because the people had not had water in days. The corporal told me that we had only enough water for ourselves. I refused the Padre's request but I felt very badly. I tried to arrange to get some water to the village as soon as we got some more.

Normandy had cost him, not his life, but much that had made it worth living. His best friends had been killed there. In the tents of the casualty clearing station he had listened to young men groan in pain that could not be relieved. The dead children haunted him. The clear moral horizon of his own being had been overshadowed by the clouds of war. He had been trying to pick up the pieces of war but often knew that he couldn't keep all the pieces together. In Normandy, the boy from the prairies found himself buffeted by violent emotions—rage, fury, hatred.

■

> I started to hate the Nazis in Normandy, and beating them pushed me to the point of exhaustion. We all enjoyed watching truckload after truckload of Nazi prisoners being taken along the Falaise road back to the coast and to a prison in England. We cheered as they went by and some of them cheered too. They seemed happy to be out of it all....

One night I stood outside the tent and shook my fist at the sky and shouted, "You'll never get me, you dirty bastards."

In the midst of all of this, Jack wrote Rita every day. He couldn't write about where they were or what they were doing but he described the people he was working with and praised the dedication of the doctors and nurses. He wrote her about Cherub, Johnny, and Ted, and about the French children. He described the installation of the new hot-water shower, and told her some of the techniques he was trying to overcome "irreversible shock". "There is a beautiful church in Cazelle that I want you to see someday," he wrote to Rita.

Rita read the letters carefully, listened to the news faithfully, and studied her maps of Normandy. Although Jack had written only that he was "somewhere in France", she was quite sure that the casualty clearing station was in the vicinity of Caen. When she was too busy to think she wrote Jack about some of the characters she worked with—like the surgeon who went around singing, "Mares eat oats and does eat oats and little lambs eat ivy", a popular song. In more reflective moments, she sent quotes from poems such as Matthew Arnold's "Dover Beach". We must be true to each other, she wrote her husband. "And we are here as on a darkling plain,...Where ignorant armies clash by night."

A few weeks after Jack left for France, the Canadian nurses had decided they would like a change from the hospital at Leatherhead. They had not minded working hard but they did not like being treated as outsiders by the British nurses. Their request for a transfer was approved and Rita was to go to a hospital in Birmingham in the fall. Before leaving, she took an August holiday with her good friend Peggy Hutton; they had been together since their crossing of the ocean in the little banana boat.

Peggy and I decided to go to Cornwall. We were exhausted and in need of a rest before going to Birmingham. We stayed in Penzance at a pleasant hotel facing the sea. We explored all the places around there and took long walks along the coastline. We sat on the cliff and looked out over the water and wondered how our husbands were. Peggy's husband was in Italy and I was sure Jack was near Caen. What was he doing?

Jack was shaking his fist at the darkened sky and shouting, "You'll never get me, you dirty bastards."

VIII

Stitches in Time

The people at the casualty clearing station began to fold their tents and leave the "killing fields" for a new field of combat. As the rest of the unit began to cross over the border between France and Belgium at the end of August, Jack was left behind for a few days to look after some of the men who couldn't be moved. It was not his finest hour. He found himself threatened with a court martial over a most grievous offence—the distribution of rum!

Jack was examining some of the patients in the ward when Corporal Dunphy came running up to say that there was a ration of rum waiting for them at the depot. The corporal asked if he could go and get it because the men had been working very hard. Jack said yes, and a good time was had by all. However, when Jack rejoined the rest of the unit he was summoned by the colonel, who said he was reporting him to General Simonds and would demand his court martial because the rum had been meant for the whole unit and not just for the small rearguard party. Fortunately another surgeon, Joe

Luke, stepped into the tent at this moment and suggested to the colonel that the punishment did not quite fit the crime.

The incident was quickly forgotten as the unit moved into Belgium. The British and Canadians were still bogged down in the Low Countries, although they had planned to be in Germany by this time. In September, the Allies had undertaken Operation Market Garden in the hope of ending the war quickly. Field Marshal Montgomery had devised a plan which was to provide the basis for a lightning strike through Belgium and Holland and into the Ruhr Valley—the industrial heartland of Germany. The strategy relied on British paratroopers and airborne divisions taking a bridge at Arnhem, in occupied Holland, and holding it until ground units could travel over the lowlands to meet them; the bridge would then give them access to Germany. Instead, the ground units got hopelessly mired in flooded areas exposed to enemy aircraft fire. Operation Market Garden was a disastrous failure, and British and Canadian troops would take another seven months to reach Germany.

As the casualty clearing station moved into Belgium it was placed under I British Corps, who were directing the battles in that area. Its first location was at Bouchout, just outside of Antwerp, at St. Gabriel's School for Boys. Antwerp was being shelled at the time and there were many snipers in the area.

On October 10 the station moved to one of its more elegant locations—a beautiful château at Brasschaat, owned by a baroness. The operating room was set up in a huge room on the main floor which had probably been the ballroom. The ceiling-to-floor windows were taped so that they could not be blown in by the V-2 rockets—faster and deadlier than the earlier V-1s—which were constantly falling around the château. Jack, who had just been placed in charge of one of the surgical teams, would operate in that ballroom until the middle of November.

In the summer of 1985, my sister and I went with Dad to visit the château at Brasschaat, which has now been converted into a five-star restaurant. As we went into the large room on the main floor, we saw crystal chandeliers hanging languidly from the ceiling, and dainty round tables covered with spotless linen, delicate candlesticks, and red roses. The large windows were clear and polished, offering an unobstructed view of the beautiful gardens beyond. It was all tinkling glass, the slight sound of silver, and the murmur of discreet service.

My father stood there for some time trying to get his bearings. He had grown comfortable with elegant restaurants, but he seemed strangely out of place and out of time in that lovely room. It was as if he was straining against the silence of history. I could only imagine what he was trying to hear: the swish of soap as he scrubbed with the assistant, the whoosh of the oxygen pump, the sawing noise as a limb was amputated, the crisp exchanges over the operating table, the sounds of shallower breathing. I couldn't see whatever it was that he was seeing—eyes straining above a surgical mask, the white gowns spattered with blood, and the raw and gaping wounds. He blinked as if he was wondering which was the mirage—what had happened then or what was happening now.

A waiter approached us and asked if we would like to see the menu. "No," said Dad, "I just wanted to see...."

As the casualties arrived at the château that fall, they were immediately processed through tents which had been set up on the front lawn as admitting and resuscitation units. Then they were taken into the operating room. As in Normandy, one of the critical problems was "irreversible shock".

> We were dealing with trauma in young and healthy men. They would arrive at the casualty clearing station with a blood pressure so low that, in spite of numerous pints of blood and plasma, they could not be made ready for surgery, and they would die. Still others would survive surgery only to die several days later after falling blood pressure and failing kidneys could not be corrected. Our thinking at that time suggested that this type of shock was irreversible for several reasons: hemorrhage, toxins, and the breakdown of the kidney function.

The weight of medical opinion today seems to suggest that such shock is almost always irreversible, although in some cases new drugs and kidney dialysis can reverse it. During the Vietnam War there were some advances in understanding how this kind of shock affects the human system. The key thing, now as then, is for treatment to begin as soon as possible.

■

> Unfortunately, in war many wounded soldiers are not brought off the battlefield for hours or even days, and then if they are in irreversible shock they cannot be saved.

Throughout the war Jack struggled to reverse this shock without a great deal of success. It was as if he and the other surgeons and nurses in the casualty clearing station were trying to reverse the shock which the war had wrought on human beings. He was fighting his own private war—not so much against the Nazis as against death itself.

If the wounded did make it to the operating room, there were other battles to fight. Often a man had been so shattered that not one but several major operations had to be performed at once if he was to have any chance of surviving. In Normandy most men had been wounded by bombs or mortar, but in Belgium and later Holland many of the wounds had been inflicted by mines left by the departing German army. Surgeons faced the challenge of saving not only life but also limbs, so that the men would not go home as permanent invalids.

One of the doctors at the station in Brasschaat was Bill Mustard, who, along with a few other surgeons, was trying new techniques in the hope of saving the legs of some of those who had been blown up by mines. He realized that if the leg's main arteries were tied the leg would often not survive, and so he decided to substitute a glass tube for the damaged main artery, as a temporary bridge to allow the circulation to continue. The patient was put on a drug called heparin to thin the blood and prevent clotting; the next day the glass tube was replaced by a section from a nearby vein, but the patient was kept on heparin for a time.

This kind of operation was not without its risks. Heparin was a tricky drug and demanded constant monitoring, which wasn't always possible because of the crush of work in the station. The heparin could cause hemorrhaging if there were other wounds. There was also the danger of infection spreading from the wound to other parts of the body.

The use of this technique was the subject of intense discussions as surgeons tried to find ways of saving the leg of the wounded man without placing his life at risk in the process. Until they could find a solution to these problems, the surgical consultants to the army recommended that this new technique be used only in carefully selected cases.

Throughout the Belgium section of Jack's diary, there are numerous notes in which he puzzles as to how some of these problems might be solved. He wrote about where the glass tubes could be placed, about the possibility of using tubes made from different materials, and about the importance of practising how to place the tubes. He wondered whether it would be helpful to place cold packs on the leg to refrigerate it so there was less pressure from the leg for a blood supply. But he never completely resolved the dilemma of saving the limb without risking the life.

■

> One afternoon when Bill Mustard was away, a man was brought in with a femoral artery injury in the leg. I started to operate with Mustard's regular assistant. However, our attempts to control the bleeding did not seem to leave us enough time to get the glass tube in place. In spite of the assistant's belief that we were nearly there, I finally called a halt and decided that we would have to amputate or the patient would die. We proceeded in this way and the patient survived.

After the war, Bill Mustard became the Chief of Cardiovascular Surgery at Toronto's Hospital for Sick Children. He was one of the first surgeons in the world to do open-heart surgery, and developed what is now called the "Mustard procedure" for transposing the great vessels of the heart in congenital heart diseases. Jack had known Mustard as a rival in hockey matches when he was at St. Michael's and Bill was at Toronto General Hospital. Their friendly rivalry continued throughout their time in the casualty clearing station—but they were always on the same side in the operating room.

Another recurrent problem they faced at the casualty clearing station was gas gangrene. Men who had lain on the ground for some time before they were picked up would assimilate bacteria from the ground through their wounds. Their muscles would become brick-red and full of gas. If this could not be corrected, amputation was inevitable.

In many cases the struggle against death was over by the time the soldiers were brought to the casualty clearing station.

■

Often, after working late into the night, I would be awakened very early in the morning with the sound of bagpipes playing a Scottish lament. When I looked out my bedroom window, I could see a single player standing outside playing the lament as several bodies of our boys were being taken off a half-ton truck and lowered into shallow graves. Our cemetery was located right next to the château. The driver of the vehicle and his helper got out of the cab of the truck and lifted the blanket-covered bodies. The blanket covered the head and most of the body but it was never long enough to cover the whole of the body. The sight of Allied army boots sticking out from under the blanket brought the reality of war home to me every morning.

Usually, these boys had been sent out in a night patrol to try to flush out German soldiers who were taking cover in the villages or in the woods. Many of the men on these patrols were from the Calgary Highlanders. Often they had to go on these patrols on a moment's notice and they had no idea where the enemy was. Waking up to the Scottish lament was like waking up to an alarm every morning.

The weather was appalling in late 1944. It was cold and wet, and in many areas the soldiers were thigh-deep in mud because the dikes had been breached. There was little to be grateful for, but Jack seems to have invested all his gratitude in a pair of rubber boots that he was issued at that time. These would remain one of his most treasured souvenirs from the war. They stood in our back hallway at home, and whenever there was a flash flood in our basement or on the street Dad would put on these boots and stride forth with commanding authority, issuing orders to his reluctant recruits.

■

> They were army issue boots, wonderfully made rubber boots, with fibre throughout them, and they were thoroughly waterproof. These boots reached up to the upper calf of the leg. They laced up from the bottom and had two clips at the top. Someone back in Canada was doing a wonderful job supplying the troops with what we really needed.

Jack wore his wonderful rubber boots to mass on Sunday morning. Padre Ed Gleason, who had been ministering to Canadian soldiers since the landing on D-Day, was saying mass in a tent, the floor of which was flooded because of all the recent rains. Jack recalls noticing that some of the men who attended the mass weren't Catholic—weren't any particular religion at all—before the war.

■

> When the time of the consecration came, I heard the sounds of splashes around me. Men were kneeling down in the water. I did too. We didn't care if we were soaked—we wanted to kneel, needed to kneel.

By mid-November, the station was moved farther into Holland. It was at that point the most forward casualty clearing station in the area, and in a particularly precarious position. Nijmegen was the focal point of the forward thrust of the Canadian and British corps, with the German army not only ahead of them but to the left and right as well. There were times when the station was in front of instead of behind the line of battle. Jack's friends teased him that, if he did not receive a letter from Rita on certain days, it meant that the Germans were behind them rather than in front of them.

The station was now located at Jonkersbosch near Nijmegen, in a building which had been a school for the mentally retarded. The Germans had used the building as a hospital when they were in control of the area and had built large airraid shelters around it. It was ideally located to receive the British, Canadian, and American casualties from the fighting raging in the area—situated as it was just off the main road to Nijmegen.

In Holland, as in Belgium and in Normandy, there were moments when the horror of war came crashing home to Jack. A face came out of the crowd of wounded and he saw another human being gazing back at him.

There was a private from Edmonton, who had been seriously wounded in his hip and abdomen. He would sit in the ward quietly singing all day long. He would sing a refrain from the song "Paper Dolly" over and over, using his forefinger as a metronome. "I'd rather have a paper doll to call my own, than have a fickle-minded real live girl." From time to time he seemed to be getting a little better but finally the infection killed him. He was just a private doing his duty, a man who wanted a paper dolly to call his own. I felt very badly when he died.

By the time Jack was in Holland, he had become an experienced surgeon and was allowed to perform most of the major operations even though he hadn't yet completed his studies.[2] However, he was beginning to feel the strain of five straight months of surgical shifts. Others were feeling the strain as well. On December 11, a lieutenant-colonel came to the station to begin proceedings against soldiers who had wounded themselves in an attempt to get out of the war. There was a whole ward of soldiers who were being treated for self-inflicted wounds.

■

I was shocked as the ward began to fill up with young men with self-inflicted wounds. Most of them had shot themselves in the toes or through one of their feet. I asked one young fellow why he had done it and he said that he had lost so many of his friends he just couldn't take it any more. He was sure that, if he didn't get out of the war, he would be killed sooner or later. He seemed happy at the thought of getting out and didn't mind the thought of a dishonourable discharge and being sent to a military prison for two years.

In fairness to these men, it should be said that most of them had never seen death before and then they had met it all of a sudden, many times over. At least we understood a little more about this kind of mental stress in World War II. In World War I when men cracked and deserted they were shot on the spot.

The only other time when Dad had to deal with such a large number of self-inflicted wounds was after he returned to Saskatoon. He kept receiving cases from the Red Earth Reserve in Northern Saskatchewan of Indians who had shot themselves in the abdomen. When he asked them why they did it they said that it was a way of getting out of the situation. They told Dad that they saw no future for themselves either on the reserve or in the white man's world.

Just before Christmas, the Germans mounted their last massive offensive in an attempt to break through the Ardennes forest and reach Antwerp—cutting off the Canadian and British troops from the rest of the Allied army. It was an extremely dangerous time.

■

> All of the officers and nursing sisters were called into the mess to hear the colonel tell us what was going on and that all the nursing sisters and married officers were to be evacuated as soon as possible. The rear party would consist of single officers and men. A number of us objected to the colonel—we were married but we didn't have children and we felt we should stay with the patients. The colonel accepted our argument. However, it was never necessary to follow through on the evacuation because the Americans stopped the Germans from breaking out to Antwerp. We were thankful we had not been put "in the bag".

In the midst of this tension, the station was visited by Professor Learmonth, a senior surgeon from Edinburgh who wanted to see the work Bill Mustard was doing on arteries. He gave some helpful suggestions to the young surgeons and also gave them an update on the war. The members of the station were not too well informed about the war going on around them, and they had to rely on visitors for some sense of the broader picture.

■

> Learmonth was sitting on one of the beds, swinging his legs and saying that the Germans were trying to break out and encircle the Canadian and American armies by outflanking them. He said we were going to be all right because we were in uniform and would be taken prisoner. However, he thought that, because he was in civilian dress, he would probably be shot as a spy. We assured him that this probably wouldn't happen.

Professor Learmonth's report on the casualty clearing station provides a helpful assessment of the work which Jack described in more modest terms. "It seemed to me that, if the patient had any chance of recovery, it was provided for him," Learmonth wrote; "the arrangements could hardly have been bettered in a teaching hospital in Britain. And certainly what were, to me, some remarkable recoveries were proceeding with a lack of incident which was equally remarkable...." He added, "Equally striking was the absorbed interest taken in their work by the medical and nursing staff. Cases were discussed and re-discussed, advice exchanged and weighed...." He was also impressed by the administration of the station: "One can only dimly conceive the immense amount of detailed thought and organization, from the highest level to the lowest, required for the attainment of such superlative results."[3]

The meeting with Learmonth would prove to be very significant for Jack. The professor asked him about his plans for after the war, and Jack replied that he hoped to go on and do a post-graduate degree specializing in surgery.

■

Learmonth said, "When you get out of the army, give me a call up in Edinburgh and I will be glad to take you on as a clinical assistant on my wards at the Royal Infirmary." It was quite a compliment and I promised him I would take him up on it.

It was the first time that Jack had started to think about more than just getting through the day's work. There were signs that the end of the war was in sight.

■

One day we walked into the mess and found a great deal of furniture—chesterfields, chairs, rugs, and small tables. We were told that this was "collaboration" stuff which had apparently been seized by the Dutch patriots since their liberation....

One Sunday a young Dutchman came to the mess and began playing the piano. He appeared very nervous and hyper. He asked us if we had any requests and we asked him to play some of the current American tunes. I asked him to play "Tea for Two" and he did, rather well. After a while he said how happy he was to see us and left. The next day we heard the Dutch military police had picked him up as a well-known collaborationist with the Germans. The chickens were coming home to roost.

Christmas 1944 was far more festive for Jack in Holland and Rita in Birmingham than it had been for years. At the casualty clearing station in Jonkersbosch, the officers and nurses served Christmas dinner to the men at noon. The meal consisted of tinned turkey with dressing and gravy.

■

> On New Year's evening our main visitor was Lieutenant-General Guy Simonds, who was commanding the Canadian army. On New Year's Day, after an excellent dinner, the men put on a skit in which they did a takeoff on Major Dewar and Captain Leddy in the operating room. Then Dewar and I had our turn doing a takeoff on privates Arbuckle and Boyce, our two highly skilled operating-room assistants. Two young Dutch girls played beautifully on the xylophone and accordion. Then sixty little Dutch girls, accompanied by their parents, danced to the music of one of the army bands. It was amazing how our unit, with the help of the Dutch civilians, was able to find such marvellous food, which was obviously in short supply, and to bring forth so much talented entertainment. Our Christmas and New Year's parties were about as good as one could find anywhere.

The hospital in Birmingham was filled with the same festive air. Rita joined the other nurses in preparing the best Christmas meal they could muster for the patients—horsemeat, potatoes, and turnips, with tinned peaches covered with tinned milk for dessert. It all seemed so deliciously extravagant.

Rita had grown very fond, not only of the servicemen in the hospital, but also of the people in the neighbourhood. The hospital was in a poorer area of the city which, because of all the factories, had been heavily damaged by a series of air raids. The rows of sooty red-brick tenements that lined the streets presented a dreary façade to someone new on the block.

However, Rita quickly discovered that this appearance was deceptive. The good humour of the people was infectious and there were several places in the neighbourhood that she began to frequent. Since there was nothing much to buy in the shops, she and some of the other nurses would spend their pocket money on plays at the repertory theatre at the bottom of the street. And if Jack had his ugly church in Mathieu, she had discovered her own beautiful church on Hagley Road—the Church of the Oratory, where John Henry Cardinal Newman had spent significant years of his life. It was the place where she felt less hungry, less weary, less alone. She could dare to feel afraid there. It was also the place where she began to think more deeply about her religion. The books and pamphlets at the back of the church stimulated her lifelong interest in Newman.

A block away from the hospital was the local pub, the focal point of the life of the neighbourhood. Rita would go there to watch the locals throw darts and play skittles and to chat over a pint. In the conversation and laughter, she felt a connection again with a community of people. She would later describe her time in Birmingham as her "Coronation Street days".

When Rita had first arrived at the hospital, she had been assigned to the emergency department—which is where the local people arrived every day in droves. Many were run down after years of poor food, cold houses, and the pressure of wartime living. She remembers one young girl who came regularly to have dressings put on her infected fingers.

> She was very pale and would come in with her infected fingers and ask, "'As it gone septic, nurse?" I soon became used to the "Brum" accent and grew to love these people....
>
> I saw this young woman one day as I looked out of the hospital window. It was cold and rainy and she was walking along the street wheeling a battered baby carriage. She had just collected her ration of coal for her fireplace. The coal was in the carriage and on top of it was a package of fish and chips wrapped in newspaper. She looked so pleased. She would have a fire in her grate that night and fish and chips for tea. It didn't take much to make her happy.

However, sadness seemed to wrap about others like a shroud. There was one nurse on staff whose eyes revealed and concealed something of the world beyond Birmingham.

> Her eyes were so large and sad and dark. We talked about many things but she was silent about herself. She said only that she was from Czechoslovakia and that she was happy her family had been able to arrange for her to come to England. She never said so but I knew she was Jewish. Every now and then she would laugh but it seemed almost by accident.

By Christmas Rita had been transferred to the men's burn unit, which had been set up especially to treat those who had been severely burned. Their recovery would be a long process—for many it would be months, for some even years, before they would recover from the searing reality of war. They would all be left with scars. Rita was amazed at the way the men bore their suffering—the burned areas of their bodies gave off a horrible smell that nothing could take away. Rita worked with a Colonel Colebrook, who was trying some new methods with penicillin cream.

There was no quick way for the burns to heal. Once the men understood that they would be in the hospital for weeks or months they settled into the routine. We would lower them into tubs of water to soak and then cover their burned areas with a change of dressing and penicillin cream.

The men called me Canada and teased me for always opening the windows. "Her likes fresh air, her does."

Visiting days were the highlight of their lives, when families would come to visit from other parts of England. They brought treats and other news from home. After these visits we had a lot of eggs which had been brought by the relatives. The patients would write their names on their eggs and I would fry them on the gas burner in the ward kitchen. Eggs were such a luxury. Sometimes a soldier would offer to give me his egg that had been brought on visiting day. I pretended I didn't like eggs. But I did! I hadn't had one since the day Jack left for France.

In early February 1945, the Canadian army was back in action. There was intense fighting as the Allies tried to flush the Germans out of the Reichswald forests. The Siegfried Line defences began to crumble and one of the British divisions broke through to Cleves. Now it was only a question of time. In early February, Jack received word that he would have a two-week leave and he was able to see Rita in Birmingham. He had a terrible chest cold at the time and was exhausted.

> After Jack arrived in Birmingham, we spent a few days in Stratford and stayed at a quaint hotel. We walked around the town and enjoyed the respite from our work—Jack's in Holland and mine in Birmingham. It had been eight months since we had seen each other and we hadn't really been able to say goodbye then.
> After a few days, his cold began to clear up. The night Jack left to return to the Continent, there was a heavy raid on Birmingham. I was staying at a hotel and all the doors along the halls opened as the guests went down to the basement in their dressing gowns. I thought how strange it would be if I were to be killed at a moment so close to the end of the war.

Upon his return to the station, Jack heard the news that two of the people in the unit had been married by the burgomaster in Turnhout, Belgium. He found their marriage vows a little different from the ones he and Rita had taken. The wife had promised to "obey the husband and not ever start any legal proceedings without the consent of the husband" and the husband had promised to "protect and allow room in his house for the wife."

By the beginning of March, the Allies were crossing the Rhine and the tactical and strategic bombing of Germany began to intensify. By the end of the month, the British and

Canadian armies had reached Muenster in the north while the Americans in the south had reached Nuremberg.

As the war was drawing to a close, Jack saw the first signs of a new era: The sky boomed as the first jet fighters flew over to Germany. A soldier took Jack out to show him the latest in weaponry—a sophisticated flame thrower.

■

> He shot the flame at a group of trees. After he was finished there was a sticky white substance hanging all over them—like spaghetti. It struck me that there wouldn't be much left of anyone who got in the way of that flame. There would be nothing I could do to help someone who was set on fire so totally.

There were fewer casualties arriving at the station. A brigadier came to instruct the staff on how to conduct themselves with German civilians. The commanders were concerned that the troops would be too kind or too cruel to the civilians on the enemy side once they were face to face.

■

> He stressed the importance of not fraternizing with Germans as we would soon be moving into their country. He pointed out that this was a firm policy of the High Command and was of the utmost importance as it was necessary to impress upon the Germans this time that they had been beaten and must pay the consequences. We were all too tired and jaded to pay much attention to this little lecture. We were more concerned with getting the war over

and getting back home. We put on a good front and our morale was a little better but we didn't take any satisfaction out of even thinking about the plight of the enemy.

At the end of March Jack took advantage of some free time to drive up to Cleves, in Germany.

■

The town was in a shambles as it had been heavily bombed by our planes. I stopped in front of a house and talked to an older German woman who seemed stunned. She tried to be friendly and took me into her house. It was a small and carefully kept house. There were some lovely cups and saucers on the shelves which seemed to have survived the shelling. Being inside her house made me think about what an average person in Germany—an old lady—had suffered because of the war. I had grown to hate the Nazis but how could I hate a nice little old lady just because she was German? She was just like all the other little old ladies in England, in France, in Belgium, in Holland.

I said goodbye to her but as I left the town it was obvious that she was one of many Germans who had seen the war brought into their homes. It wasn't a delight to see their depression.

Many years later, in Jerusalem, my sister Jennifer met a young German woman from the Ruhr Valley by the name of Julie Kirchberg. The two of them became good friends. Jennifer grew to appreciate the language of her friend and they spoke for hours about their hopes and dreams. For my sister, German was a language of friendship and of peace.

I was forced to study German in the course of my graduate research on the history of the Holocaust. To me, it was the language of Hitler's rantings, the language of war and of hatred. It was not a language I wanted to learn. The only exam I ever failed was German. I failed it four times before a professor finally gave me a pass for persistence.

Our lives are deeper and longer than we know. My sister had arrived at my father's acceptance of real German people while I had been left with his resistance to the ideology of Nazism. Fortunately, my sister and I talk a lot together. German, like English or any other language, is a language of war and of peace.

In the spring of 1945, signs began to appear everywhere saying, "Kilroy was here." Sometimes the sign would include a picture of a bald-headed man with a big nose looking over a fence. Jack noted that the slogan was oddly comforting.

■

> We didn't know what it meant but it felt reassuring. It seemed to mean somebody else had passed over the ground we were on and had survived. Next to "I love you" the next most important three words in the war were "Kilroy was here."

IX

Small Victories

The war bestowed one small departing blessing on Jack and Rita. After months of separation, they would be together on VE Day.

In early May 1945, Jack received orders to transfer back to #24 General Hospital at Horley in England. There was a farewell party for him in the casualty clearing station. The staff, which had begun as a rather odd collection of people, was now a team. In the heat of many moments, they had come to know each other at their worst and at their best. They couldn't consider themselves a winning team—there were too many losses for that—but they had stayed in the field. For many on staff, their service in the station would stand as their finest experience of being involved in a community of purpose.

The war in Italy was over. One by one the cities of Germany had fallen. Hitler had committed suicide on April 30. Berlin had fallen on May 3. That was the day Jack left for England, sitting on the back of a motorcycle behind a British soldier who drove at top speed through the wind and rain to Brussels.

From there, Jack hitchhiked to Ostend. As he waited for his boat, he jotted another entry in his diary:

■

> May 5, 1945: Late Saturday night. Sitting on the dock at Ostend waiting to push off for England and for Rita.

It had been nine months since he had crossed the Channel for the first time. Was it really only nine months? It was as if he had crossed over into a strange world and was now returning to a world which was no longer so familiar. He needed to be back with Rita to discover his bearings again.

As soon as the ferry docked he took a train north and reported to the hospital at Horley. Once his work was settled, he asked for and was granted a short leave.

■

> I left as early as I could on May 8. I had to switch trains for Birmingham in London. It was still foggy when I got out on the platform but I could hear church bells starting to ring. It was then that I knew the war was over. Men on the platform started yelling at me and I yelled back—"The war is over!" The bells were ringing, more and more, louder and louder. People started flowing out onto the streets, some of them still in their pyjamas. I took the next train to Birmingham and ran over to the hospital to get Rita, who was waiting at the front door for me.

> The first thing we did was to go over to the church on Hagley Road. We went to pray in thanksgiving—because we were alive, because the war was over. We prayed for all of those who had died during the war. Then we went over to the room we had rented, opened a bottle of champagne, and had our own celebration.

Rita could hardly believe her eyes when she saw Jack running up to the hospital through all the crowd that was gathering in the street.

> People were out in the streets laughing and crying and embracing one another. I was so happy but I couldn't jump for joy. We had been married since 1941 and now, four years later, the war was over. Yes, it was finally over. There had been too many hopes dashed, too much waiting, too much worrying, too much death and too little food. It had taken so much to arrive at this day. Victory in Europe! It would take some getting used to. Could it be true? Yes...it was true. It was over. Now our lives could begin.
> Jack said, "Let's have lots of children right now." It was as if he wanted to forget about all the death and destruction and get on with life.

After a few days in Birmingham, Jack returned to Horley. He discovered that it was a place for people in transit—as he himself was in transit. He was not exactly sure of his future. There was some possibility that, after a leave, he would be sent over to the Pacific front.

■

> Some were going over to Europe to be part of the Army of Occupation and others, like myself, were returning from Italy or north-west Europe. Some of the administrators of the hospital had just arrived from Canada and were frustrated at not having had the opportunity of serving with a medical unit in action. It seemed to me that they were on the defensive. They found it difficult to understand our deep fatigue, our mental and physical exhaustion. They would not give us the leave on weekends that we thought we needed. They were reacting—and we were reacting!
>
> However, on the whole the unit was quite happy, and we would spend many hours in the mess after a day's work telling stories about all the experiences we had been through during the war. We talked about the news that was coming out of Germany about the concentration camps. It was shocking but, somehow, not surprising.

Jack's fatigue was not something that could be remedied with a few hours of rest. No one was sure what the cure was for "combat fatigue". Jack would go to visit Rita but he was almost too tired to talk, too tired to listen.

By the summer, Rita and Jack knew that they were going to be parents. Jack noted in his diary, "We are expecting Junior in February 1946." Rita felt within herself that this was their new beginning. She quit her job in Birmingham and moved to Smallfield, a little village near Horley.

I had a pleasant time there living with Mr. and Mrs. Coste in their house called Covertside. At first they served me my meals in my room but then they discovered that I was a bookworm and they invited me to have meals with them. The three of us would go into the dining room with our books and prop them up on the table. We read all the way through our meals. It was a great change from hospital dining rooms. I read most of Jane Austen that summer.

I went with them to country fairs and played whist with them and their friends. There was such a relaxed feeling and everything was so quiet. We didn't have to worry about bombings. The food was still scarce and there were the eternal "queues" in the little shops but we managed.

Jack came over to visit as often as he could. We would sit on the swing in the garden of Covertside. He would sleep and I would read.

For Jack, as for Rita, peace took some getting used to. They could begin to look up at the sky without fear. They could begin to hear themselves think.

During that summer in England, I couldn't get over how quiet the nights were in and around the London area. There were no air raids, no bombs dropping, no rockets flying in from out of nowhere, no stricken aircraft struggling to keep aloft. I loved the long summer evenings with no blackout. Rations were still poor and everyone looked gaunt and tired but there was a sense of relief.

They started to relax a little that peaceful summer together—but not completely. There was still the open question of where Jack would be sent next. In early August, their greatest anxiety was relieved with the news of the surrender of Japan. A new and different anxiety emerged briefly around the edges of their consciousness. Jack was preoccupied with thoughts about the victims of the bombings of Hiroshima and Nagasaki. He remembered the people he had seen ripped apart by smaller bombs and wondered about the condition of those who had been exposed to so much heat and radiation.

■

> When I heard the news of Hiroshima, I felt quite ill and nauseated. I thought—what a dreadful weapon. Where will it all end?

Rita was just returning from her first prenatal visit when she saw a rain-drenched newspaper lying in the ditch beside the bus stop. The headline screamed: "Japan Surrenders!" All she knew was that she and Jack could finally begin to plan for the future.

Jack came over to Covertside and they began to talk about the various options which were open to them. Jack's career was not the only concern; Rita was feeling weak and they wanted her to get some better nourishment before the baby was born. They weighed the offer that Professor Learmonth had extended to Jack back in Holland, to take Jack on as a clinical assistant. That would give Jack the opportunity to do his fellowship in surgery at the University of Edinburgh, one of the finest schools in the world. Both Jack and Rita knew that they would not be able to afford that possibility once they were back in Canada. The three thousand dollars or so that Jack would receive in re-establishment credit would not allow him to start a practice in Canada and then go back to Scotland. Rita knew Jack could no more not be a surgeon than not be himself. They talked long into the night.

> Finally we decided that I should return to Canada to have our child and that Jack would go to Edinburgh alone to prepare for the fellowship exam. Jack felt sure that he would be ready for the exam with two months' study. We went up to Whitehall together and the authorities arranged to get me a passage home.

In October, Jack took Rita down to Avonmouth, near Bristol. They were able to work it so that Rita and her friend Peggy Hutton would be on the same vessel. It was another banana boat! It was also another farewell.

The crossing was far less dangerous this time, but Rita was not feeling as well as she had on the first trip. The year and a half of civilian rations and the pregnancy made her more vulnerable to seasickness. Most of the time she couldn't make it to the dining room; all she could eat were oranges (a luxury at the time) and peppermint patties. She never liked peppermint patties after that.

Rita shared a cabin with three English war brides who were leaving their families to join their husbands in Canada. They were somewhat apprehensive about what they would face in this new country. Although Rita was leaving her husband behind, she was excited about her return.

> As we were going up the St. Lawrence River to Montreal, we stood on the deck and looked at the lovely French villages and the beautiful maple trees. England had been beautiful too but we were Canadians and this was home. Canada seemed so big after England—and so bright. We were fascinated by Montreal—there were no bombed-out areas and there was so much food. We caught our trains there—Peggy to Calgary and I to Oshawa.

Because there were not enough boats to take all the servicemen back to Canada immediately, the Canadians in the forces had to wait their turn to return to Canada or even to be demobilized. Jack continued to work at Horley. His turn for discharge came on December 10, 1945. He left the army ranked as a major.

■

> It was a strange feeling when the senior officer who gave me my discharge stood up and shook my hand and thanked me on behalf of Canada for my service.
>
> I went back to the hospital and changed into civilian dress. It was a utility suit that I had picked up somewhere. It was a little baggy but at least I was dressed to begin life again.

The last entry in Jack's diary is on this day: "Happy to be out. I have had more than enough."

He left for Edinburgh and went to see Professor Learmonth, and was put to work immediately as clinical assistant to Learmonth on his wards at the Royal Infirmary. The professor's secretary, Miss Norrie, gave Jack a room in her house and did everything possible to make him feel at home. He spent Christmas that year with Professor Learmonth's family and even learned a few Scottish dances in the course of the evening.

Right after Christmas, Jack began to prepare for the fellowship exam. He was told that he should be ready to be examined on "anything relating to surgery". Although he knew that most people took one or two years to study for this exam, he felt what he had learned during the war would stand him in good stead.

He underestimated the effect of his combat fatigue.

■

> It was a big change to go back to the books. I lacked concentration. I couldn't work at anything for very long. I would try to read but I would feel the need to sleep after an hour. I would sleep for half an hour and then read for another hour before falling asleep again. I felt weak most of the time.

Nevertheless, he was so anxious to get back to Rita that he tried the exam in late January—and failed. He was not the only one—all the young surgeons who had been in the war, the brightest and the best (like Bill Bigelow and Bill Mustard), failed. After the bad news, though, came the good news. Rita telegraphed him that their daughter, Mary Jo, had been born on February first. Jack was delighted and told everyone at the hospital who would listen, and then he went to find Miss Norrie, who was planning a special meal for the day the baby arrived. She had been saving her money to buy a bottle of champagne for the celebration.

Spurred on by this good news, Jack tried desperately to concentrate enough to write the exam again in March. He failed again. It was one of his darkest moments, a moment when he personally felt quite defeated by the war. All he wanted to do was pack it in and go home to Rita.

Andrew Lowdon, a junior staff surgeon who had been one of the examiners, came to see him and Jack told him he just wanted to go home as soon as possible.

■

> Andrew told me that my work was very good but he could see that I was exhausted. "Your handwriting is terrible," said Andrew, "the other examiners commented on it—obviously you're still exhausted from the war." Andrew asked me if I had called my wife. I said that I hadn't because I couldn't afford it. I was going to telegraph her about my return. Andrew said, "I think you should call your wife. You can't afford not to."
>
> I called Rita and she wept quietly when I told her the bad news. There was silence for what seemed like a very long time. Then she told me that I should get some rest, a holiday, and some good food, and try again. It was good advice and I took it.

Rita put down the phone and sobbed into the night. Would the war ever be over for them? She had returned to Canada thinking that her husband would soon be home as well. She had gone through the labour and birth of their child alone. Her only way of being close to Jack in those hours had been to go back to St. Michael's Hospital for the delivery—back to where they had begun together. And now she felt she would be alone for what seemed like for ever.

The cries of their baby called her out of this darkness. There were diapers to be washed, bottles to be boiled. Rita contacted her cousins and rejoined the Oshawa Public Library—where she had first become a member in Grade 1. She read her way through the poetry section in the following months.

Jack took a full year to prepare for his next attempt at the exam. He went for a long holiday to Wales and spent some time at various hospitals in London. On the third try, he passed the exam with flying colours and started to pack for home. He telegraphed Rita in April 1947 that he had booked passage on a freighter—giving her the name of the freighter and telling her it would be docking in New York in a few weeks. His plan was to phone from New York and then take the train to Oshawa.

Rita decided to surprise Jack and go down to New York to meet him. Because Jack was not travelling on a passenger ship, she had no idea when or where he would be arriving, but she was determined to find out. Rita's mother was glad to look after the baby but she was more worried about her daughter going to New York than she had been when she had left for Europe!

The bank manager in Oshawa had got Rita a room at the Belmont Plaza Hotel, and as soon as she arrived she set off in search of her husband.

I phoned around to all the freighting companies until I found out when the ship would be arriving and where. It was down at the 25th Street dock in the warehouse area and I went down there the morning of that day I knew Jack would be arriving.

> I saw Jack before he saw me. He was standing on the deck as the ship pulled into the harbour—looking so pale and tired. He was wearing a wartime suit which didn't fit him and a woollen scarf that had a big hole in it. He looked like a refugee! Where was my dapper Major Leddy!

Jack could see someone waving wildly on the dock. As the ship drew closer he was overwhelmed to realize that it was Rita.

■

> There she was. I was amazed and thrilled at her courage—standing with all those tough dock workers. She hadn't changed a bit. The plank was lowered and finally I could hold her. She had obviously told the men all about me because they offered to carry my trunk and said, "Welcome home, Major." I was home.

They returned to Oshawa after a few days together in New York. Almost immediately they moved to Hamilton, where Jack began working at the McGregor Clinic. In the evenings, they would discuss Jack's operations and how some of the techniques he had learned in the war were proving useful in cases of shock. Jack was still exhausted at the end of each day but he was slowly regaining his strength.

Their second daughter, Jennifer, was born in Hamilton on January 4, 1949. Shortly after that, Jack's father died in Saskatoon. While Jack was out west, Rita phoned him and begged him to come home. It was the only time she had ever made such a request and Jack, sensing that something was very wrong, returned as quickly as he could. She had become terribly ill after Jennifer's birth but the doctors told her it was only a case of nerves. Jack told the doctors, "I know what she has been through and she has never had a case of nerves." He ordered a series of X-rays and they revealed a large abscess over one of her kidneys. The operation took place just in time.

While Rita was recovering, Jack was informed that there was an opening for a Chief of Surgery at St. Paul's Hospital in Saskatoon. Rita and Jack knew that they would soon have to decide on where to settle down. They decided on Saskatoon.

My father needed to go back to the prairies. I think my mother knew that. Even if it meant uprooting herself from the relationships that had sustained her, the move held the promise of her husband standing on his own ground again.

It would not always be easy for them in Saskatoon. On the cocktail circuit, the subject of the war was off limits except as a joking matter. In the small medical circles, the doctors who had not been overseas made much of all the work they had had to do during the war. Rita found it exasperating to hear other wives lament about how difficult it had been to get shoes during the war. Jack joined the Riverside Golf and Country Club only to find, to his dismay, that it was still almost impossible for Jews to get membership there. There were times when it seemed as if the war had never happened.

But life picked up Rita and Jack and threw them forward. Their wartime equipment, letters, and the diary were placed in a trunk in the attic. Jack put all of his energy into establishing a practice and Rita was completely absorbed by home, school, and parish. A third child, Michael, was really the son of their peacetime lives.

Their struggles were those of most couples—struggles which were far easier and yet more difficult than the ones they had gone through during the war. There were the petty politics of the medical world, rearguard actions with the bank, their own battles and truces. Life with three children was often far from peaceful.

Every now and then, my father would buy the latest book about the history of the war and would sit with it in his den, trying to comprehend the larger story of which he and Mom had been a part. He rarely had time to finish the book.

Yet he had time to go back to the nearby town of Delisle. One of the things he always insisted on was that we go to help his old friends the Bentleys with the harvest in the fall. Mom preferred to stay inside the house and chat with some of the women and men, just as she had gathered with her relatives back in Oshawa the day war was declared. We would go out with Dad and ride the truck behind the combine.

He would stretch his hand out to the sky and say to us, "Look at that sky. That's a good sky."

And it was—very good.

Epilogue

A World of Difference

I took the story of Jack and Rita Leddy for granted as I was growing up—just as I took my own life and the world itself for granted. Now it is different. I have shared their memories of war long enough to return to myself with this sureness: the less I take for granted, the more I want to promise.

Perhaps I took the story of my parents for granted because it seemed so, well, ordinary. Not the stuff of high drama or momentous history. The moderately happy ending had cast a certain light over their whole story. I had yet to see the shadowed moments when the ending seemed far from certain for them. I had missed the thousand moments of fear, of courage, of fidelity and love beyond reason. I had read so many other stories from the Second World War which had such horrible endings that I had missed the meaning of the experience of my own parents.

The story of Jack and Rita Leddy is not about greatness but about goodness, not about great goodness but about genuine goodness. This is why it bears retelling.

There has been a great deal written about the evildoers who thrived during the Nazi era. Some attempt has been made to analyse why some people commit crimes of great magnitude. Yet there has been relatively little reflection on the lives of those who brought a measure of goodness in that dark time. It seems sad but true that we are often more horrified or fascinated by evil than amazed at goodness and attracted by it.

My parents' memories merge into one small story of goodness. There are many other such stories—most of them too long untold. There are voices in time which should not be taken for granted, which should not remain silent for want of our words to retell their stories.

If I have allowed myself to feel some amazement about my own mother and father, it is not out of a blind sense of devotion but rather because of my desire to see goodness wherever it may be found. I have written many other stories about pure and simple goodness but this is the one I now know most intimately. It was written in my heart long before it came to mind.

As I was writing this story, I realized that dimensions of my parents had become married inside of me. The man of action, the woman of words, had given birth to my own conviction that writing and speaking were my ways of acting in the world. Because of them, I wanted to conceive of words that were more life-giving than death-dealing. I discovered within me the seed of their love, which took root as persistent hope in moments when words seemed to wither and action proved fruitless.

Yet I also understood that their story had a meaning beyond myself. Jack and Rita Leddy are not only my parents, they are a brother and a sister in our human journey, two children of the past, two grandparents of the future. We do well to wonder what their memories mean for us, here and now.

I have searched through my parents' story for clues as to why their goodness seemed almost second nature in a time defined by war and diminished by hatred. My search, as I had anticipated, yielded no conclusive evidence to support a theory about human behaviour. One should not generalize on the basis of the experience of two people. The story of Jack and Rita Leddy would be stretched beyond the limits of its reality if it were used as the basis for a sustained treatise about war, peace, or whatever.

Yet, while a particular human experience discloses less than everything about life, it may still reveal more than nothing. Something remains to be said. As we approach the end of this violent century, a period of history in which evil has had more than its day, we can ill afford not to explore even the tentative and partial truths of a single story of goodness.

As I turn over the pages of my parents' story in my mind, I see that goodness was not so much an ideal they aspired to as a reality they had experienced. They were neither grimly moralistic nor obsessively responsible. They delighted in dancing, enjoyed their work, appreciated their country, cherished their friendships, and rejoiced in each other. Life was more promising than problematic for them.

After the war broke out, they gradually realized that everything promising in their lives was threatened by the Nazi design for domination. In the end, it seems that they joined in the war effort not so much because of what they were *against* but because of what they were *for*. They were more for life than against the machinery of death, more for truth and freedom than against the perverse propaganda and tyranny of the Nazi regime. They were too much in love not to recognize the menace of hatred and violence, too much in love to define their lives only in terms of being against such viciousness.

My own involvement in various social and political struggles leads me to confirm the importance of defining one's life in positive terms. It is all too easy to become like that which one is fighting against. Such a stance, I have learned, is not without its risks. In the long, hard struggle against bureaucratic injustices, some social activists begin to sort and classify other people according to their usefulness to a cause. In fighting against Communism, there are those who begin to bypass democratic procedures in the name of national security. It matters which mirrors we hold up to our lives.

My parents reflected back to each other the promise of love and the desire for peace. I suppose this is why they emerged from the war somewhat bruised but not broken. Peace appeared as a blessing for them because they saw themselves through the eyes of someone who loved them. Being in love, Jack and Rita were less tempted to romanticize war. They did not need to flirt with death in order to feel more alive. If they resisted the coercive power of the enemy, it was only because they had experienced the irresistible power of love.

The reality of war drew a line between everything my parents had taken for granted and everything they would be for ever grateful for. The war was their harshest reminder that what was promising in life was not necessarily guaranteed. After 1939, they never took justice or freedom for granted again. They recognized that such ideals could only be realized through the efforts of countless ordinary people such as themselves. The guarantee could not be written in ink alone. It had to be underlined with real commitments, spelled out in everyday life, punctuated with exclamations of human hope.

And Jack and Rita never took their love for each other for granted. They never quite got over their amazement at being together. Almost fifty years of marriage have allowed them to presume on each other, but they have never taken being alive and together for granted.

I am beginning to realize how profoundly I have been shaped by their shared sense of gratitude for life. As the years pass, it becomes more evident to me that not everyone acts out this simple sense of gratitude.

There are those who do good more out of a sense of guilt than out of gratitude. Guilt may galvanize us into action for a while. But not for long, not for a lifetime. Guilt may stop us from doing wrong but it does not sustain us in doing good. Although it may result in a spasm of reaction, it eventually becomes an immobilizing cramp. For example, the guilty awareness that one *has* too much is often accompanied by the fear that one *is* too little. The sense that others do not have enough often reflects back on oneself and is internalized as the feeling "I am not enough" or "We are not enough." If we look long enough only at what is bad in the world, we begin to see ourselves as not being good enough. Guilt does not nourish giving but gnaws away at the soul of our concern for the world, leaving us consumed as persons in the process.

For those who are grateful, the bottom line of life is a blessing rather than a burden. Gratitude for what has been given is really the starting point for a life which is given over to others. Gratitude enables us to recognize what is promising in life. It is the ground from which we grow in a desire to make a promise of our own lives—to others and to the world.

Such an attitude is more than gratefulness for this or that thing, this or that person, this or that moment. It is the simple awareness that just being alive is an amazing grace, a gift we could never manage on our own. This is such a simple awareness, yet the one most easily obscured, because we tend to take the fact of being alive for granted. When I contemplate the series of events that led to my parents' reunion on VE Day, I am shaken by the realization that any change in those circumstances would have meant that I would never have been born.

Most of us spend a lot of time wishing things had been or could be a little different in our lives. We add up the pluses and minuses of the past and do a cost/benefit analysis of the future. We miss the amazing fact that we even have a life to moan and muse about.

To appreciate the fact that one has been given the immeasurable gift of life makes one more sensitive to the tragedy of squandering life, hoarding it, or measuring it out in little pieces. While the guilty person measures life in terms of who has more and who has less, who is better and who is worse, the grateful person is more given to living generously, not counting the cost.

I think Mom and Dad realized that their love for each other would be compromised if they hoarded or cautiously measured out their gifts of healing. They knew that their profession held out the promise of life for those who were wounded or dying. Yet there were doctors and nurses at that time whose skills were used more in the service of death than of life. Some Nazi doctors were willing to make a sacrifice of the lives of others in the interests of science. There is all the difference in the world between a doctor who views another person merely as an object to be experimented upon and a doctor who sees the human body as the bearer of infinite promise, between a nurse who treats life like a possession and a nurse who has allowed herself to be possessed by life.

There was a moment when my parents' memories of the wounded evoked an image that was already half-formed within my own memory. In my mind's eye, I could see my father's hands as they quickly moved to close a wound, my mother's hands as she gently removed the dressing from a burn. In a moment of revelation, they appeared to me as menders of the world.

The image of "mending the world" first surfaced for me during a philosophy class with Professor Emil Fackenheim at the University of Toronto. He explained that, in the Jewish tradition, *tikkun ha olam* meant to mend, to repair, to transform the world. It was a term that felt a little foreign but, at the same time, somewhat familiar.

The image of mending the world took me back to some early family memories: my mother mending our clothes in the evenings—and we did tear through quite a lot of clothes in the course of our childhood. In fact, mending would probably feel like an essentially feminine activity to me were it not for my awareness of my father's work. When other kids used to ask me what he did, I said, "He sews people up."

I learned some early lessons about mending the world. From my mother, I learned the importance of selecting threads with the right tensile strength, the ones appropriate for the fabric to be mended. I learned that things become worn out and threadbare in the normal course of life, that mending is an ordinary everyday activity to be attended to.

From my father, I learned that mending is often a matter of life and death. That if the wound is too deep, there will be a scar left even after the mending has taken place.

From both my parents, I got the sense that mending was not an essentially creative task, but rather an activity of care and commitment. In mending one works with what is given, with what is ripped and torn and wounded. However, mending is more than putting a patch on things and covering over that which has come apart. Mending begins only after there is an awareness that something has been ripped. It is an activity of restoring so that, as my mother used to say, it looks "almost like new".

I learned from my parents (and later from my own experience) that not all stitches hold, that not every wound can be fully healed. Yet I have come to understand that the process of mending is what holds together the fabric of life. Without such mending, our lives would be threadbare of promise, coming apart at the seams.

These early images of mending have helped me to understand how the social fabric is held together through the activities of justice and the works of mercy.

The social fabric is weakened whenever and wherever people are weakened through an unequal relationship of dominance and dependence. There were and are many instances of this pattern of relating: between rich and poor, black and white, men and women, natives and newcomers, Jews and Christians. The process of transforming these relationships along more equal lines is the labour of justice.

Not everyone sees the injustice perpetuated through such patterns of inequality. For some, that is simply the way life was, is, and always will be. They have no awareness that it could be any different, no desire to make it any different. Perhaps doubting whether they can make any difference in the world, they cannot allow themselves to see, to feel, the injustice.

I am not sure what it is that moves some people to want to strengthen the threads of human justice. It may be another person who becomes a whole world to us. Perhaps a face comes out of the crowd and we come face to face with ourselves. Or perhaps we begin to see the world through the eyes of children, from the perspective of the most innocent victims of injustice. Then again, it may be the disturbing and wonderful biblical dream handed on through generations of believers—a dream of wholeness which seems stronger than the fact of brokenness in the world.

In any case, the process of transforming social relationships is a long and difficult task. Because social inequalities can only be maintained by overt or subtle forms of violence, it can seem as if the only way of changing these relationships of dominance and dependence is through equally violent means. But the only peace that is possible within a situation of radical injustice is the peace of the dead. Even the victories of war bring only a temporary halt to the long reign of violence in the world. Ultimately, enduring peace must be rooted in a condition of justice, in a situation in which the equality of each person and all peoples is socially and politically guaranteed.

When the fabric of social justice comes apart at the seams, when the pattern of peace is broken, then mending the world takes the form of merciful response. The work of Jack and Rita Leddy during the war was essentially one of mercy. Together with many others, they attempted to rescue people whose bodies had borne some of the brunt of a war started by those who saw themselves as a race without equal.

Nevertheless, the stories of the merciful can never be completely consoling. While Jack and Rita were able to help some live a little longer and a little better, there were many more who died beyond the reach of anyone. Mercy helps to sustain the promise of human life but it is justice which provides its strongest guarantee.

My parents, however, were far more than menders of the world; they were also lovers and friends. In the mending that was their work, they attended to the wounded in a worn-out world. In loving each other, they entered into a whole new world of promise. While their work was often redemptive, it was their love which was creative.

The moments of creation in life are those new beginnings that could never have been planned or anticipated. As "in the beginning", love and friendship are miracles we could never have manufactured. Beauty lights unexpectedly, truth surfaces from somewhere out of sight, and goodness gleams suddenly like a gold tooth in a widening smile. Only in retrospect can we take this all for granted. The future always opens within us as a freshness.

Those who act justly and mercifully help to lay the groundwork for love and friendship and all that is promising in this world. When people stand on an equal footing, they are more likely to reach out in love and friendship.

There are certain social and political conditions that make love and friendship not inevitable but more possible. Love and friendship flourish between equals (and being equal does not mean being the same) and flounder in the artificial distances created by divisions of race or class. Love and friendship take root more easily when there is the possibility of tomorrow, when the future is not placed in jeopardy, when life is not reduced to the concerns of the present moment by the constant struggle to eke out an existence.

Peace, too, makes love and friendship more possible. Not every relationship emerged intact from the wreckage of the Second World War. Some relationships could not span the distance of separation; others could not survive the crippling effects of injury. In one way or another, the war dealt a death blow to many a relationship.

Nevertheless, it is important to claim the possibility of love and friendship on even the shakiest of grounds, at even the most perilous of times. Love can bloom in the smallest space as long as that space is sure. Jack and Rita Leddy claimed a space for love in the midst of a world ground up by war. My own involvement in the struggles for justice and peace leads me to affirm the love and friendship which are within the bounds of possibility. So often a better world seems beyond our reach. It will be a very long time before the world becomes a place of promise, of justice, peace, and freedom for all. In the meantime, we need to stand in a small and sure space of love which will help us keep sight of the horizon of our hopes.

Unfortunately, there are those who have lost sight of a broader social hope. Abdicating responsibility for the wider world, they turn their attention to the small world over which they have some control—the home front, the arena of work and play. Some have focused their efforts on developing the one world that seems truly their own—the world of the self. But the smaller world of personal life soon becomes inflated and distorted. Taking peace for granted, these people find themselves engaged in petty soap-opera wars fuelled by jealousy and competition; taking freedom for granted, they come to think of it as the range of choice on the shelves of the supermarket; taking justice for granted, they act as if equality meant dressing in the same way as everyone else, having the same cars, listening to the same music.

My parents never lost sight of their responsibility to the larger public world—perhaps because they were never blind to the reality of a far deeper world. In the dark nights when death held dominion over those around them, they reached out to reclaim the strand of spirit that connected them to God. When the reality of war threatened to overwhelm any promise of peace, they realized that the thread of their lives, no matter how long or how strong, had its limits. At the times when I have been up against the powers that be, I have had my own stark realization that, even if we can help to lengthen and strengthen the lives of others through the work of justice and mercy, none of these threads will hold for ever. The thread of promise in the world ultimately relies on a divine promise. However, this is not a promise that God can make in our absence. I suspect that God does not take our mending of the world for granted.

In some ways, I continue to dwell in the world of my parents. Yet there is at least one significant way in which I live in a different world. I was born as the mushroom cloud was casting its shadow over the earth. The dropping of the atom bomb on Hiroshima and Nagasaki has made all the difference in the world. My ground is more than shaky. I can no longer take even the earth for granted.

Until 1945, human beings could take at least the earth for granted. It was solid ground, the place, we presumed, where people would continue to be born and to die, where wars would be won and lost, where empires would rise and fall. No one ever said it was a perfect place or the end of the road but it was a good place to begin—the only place to begin. When people have a place to begin, they can start to wonder where it will all end up.

My parents' memories have helped me to think about, to have feelings about, the last great war. However, I become almost numb at the thought of the next world war—which will surely be the war to end all wars. We human beings were not created to cope with the thought of the holocaust of millions of people in half an hour. Our minds and hearts were not created to grasp such a monstrous possibility. We simply cannot imagine our city vaporized in seconds. We cannot feel the irradiation of one person we love—much less two...or three. Our hearts and minds were made for so much more, and so much less, than this.

So...we bury ourselves in business as usual, life as usual, religion as usual. We try to forget that the unthinkable has become the possible. Mindless activism can be a race from the thought of the world stopping. Cool professionalism can be an insulation against the burning issues of the day. Single-issue concerns can be a refuge from the fact that everything is now at issue.

Those who struggle to think about the possibility of nuclear war can often only conceive of it in terms borrowed from the experience of the Second World War. The story of the particular war that dominated my parents' generation has so shaped our consciousness of war in general that we hardly know how to think about war in any other way. We are used to thinking of a war in which there are winners and losers. Because we were so obviously on the side of right in the struggle against the Axis powers, we assume that we would be on the side of right in any future war. The Second World War has also, unfortunately, made us all too familiar with the manufacture of mass murder. Auschwitz and Hiroshima have become precedents for nuclear war—the final solution of the human race.

We are unable to think about, unable to imagine, unable to feel what we are none the less able to do—to destroy the earth and the human race. This remains true in spite of the encouraging steps which have been taken recently to reduce the nuclear arms arsenal. War, by accident or design, is a continuing threat as long as two nuclear weapons continue to hold the earth hostage. Even if it is difficult to think about nuclear war, it has never been more necessary to do so.

In a nuclear war, there would not be any winners but only losers. The bomb would fall on the good and bad alike, on young and old, men, women, and children. The distinction between military targets and civilian populations, which became increasingly blurred in the mass bombings of the Second World War, would be erased in a nuclear holocaust. There would be no meaningful sacrifice or courage; there would be no time for it. The war would be fought not in years but in minutes. In such an inferno, there would be neither heroes nor villains, only survivors—and the living might well envy the dead.

As long as we install nuclear weapons in the heart of our western culture, we are harbouring the thought, consciously or unconsciously, of the possibility of killing millions of human beings. A moral numbness is setting into our souls. We are being spiritually and psychologically deadened, even if a bomb never drops. We are beginning to take death—not death from natural causes but humanly executed death—for granted.

Everything depends on our acting "in time" to prevent the next, last, world war. My parents taught me some early lessons about the importance of responding "in time" to critical situations. My mother pointed out that "a stitch in time saves nine". My father explained that one had to move very quickly to prevent a patient from going into irreversible shock. I conclude that, if one does not act in time, then the moment passes and the situation is soon beyond repair.

In my studies of the history of the Second World War, I was struck by how many people did not act "in time" to stop the Nazis. There were so many signs of the Nazis' dark designs in the thirties for those who wished to see them. Some, in Europe, Canada, and elsewhere, recognized the signs of danger but remained silent because they did not see themselves as endangered. Few in Germany protested as the rights of the Jews and others were slowly but surely suspended to the point of extinction. And then the time for non-violent protest was over. The tanks rumbled across Europe and the trains began their transports to the death camps.

There are hundreds of volumes documenting the evils that were done by the Nazis. Yet there is still much to be said about what so many good and nice people of that time did not do. For Mr. and Mrs. Normal, Professor Normal, and the normal worker, it was business as usual, church as usual, and home sweet home. So many seem to have abdicated a sense of responsibility for public life and enshrouded themselves in the tiny private world of personal purpose. The Nazis did not have to seize political power in Germany—they found it lying in the streets and they picked it up. Soon the walls surrounding private lives began to crumble, in Germany and elsewhere, as the menace of Nazism gained momentum.

One would think that the memories of Jack and Rita Leddy and millions of others would move us to act "in time" against any threat of war. Yet memories alone do not always serve us well. War continues to hold out its dark and illusory promises for many. Conventional wars continue unabated in many parts of the world and seem acceptable, even comfortably familiar, after what happened in the Second World War. There are daily news reports of body-count politics. "Nuclear deterrence" has become a terrifyingly normal term.

Memories of war do not serve us well if we see no connection between what happened in the past and what is happening now. This disconnection of the past from the present is as disconcerting as the way in which contemporary societies are organized so that we see little connection between present actions and future consequences. Within the bureaucratic organization of our society, many people have become insulated from the consequences of their own actions. Our social systems create the conditions through which nice and ordinary people can contribute to evil results without even realizing it. With nodding heads, the committee members bow to economic necessity. With fingertip control, a secretary types out the memo. With the stroke of a pen, an executive eliminates the funding for refugees, the unemployed, the people of a village in the third world. With a flick of the wrist, a clerk files away the cries for reconsideration. Nobody within the system feels responsible for this wreckage of human lives. Nobody has to face the tired eyes, the desperate eyes, of those who will bear the brunt of this systematic decision. A system renders its workers shockproof against the claims of reality.

None of us is foolproof in this regard. We all participate in one system or another: economic, social, political, educational, or even religious. The greatest illusion is to think that we can do no wrong simply because we are ordinary or nice or well meaning. It is an illusion to think that we Canadians are peaceful people simply because we do not possess such weapons. In fact, we make the parts for Cruise missiles, send them south, and then welcome back the assembled missiles on their test flights north.

Canadians are particularly prone to this illusion of innocence. Our selective remembrance of our own history has made us less sensitive to its repetitive patterns in the present. While we are ready to recall the heroic Canadian resistance against Nazism, we tend to overlook the injustices closer to home during that period. We should not forget that the Canadian government closed its doors to Jews fleeing from Europe, and that Japanese Canadians were interned as "enemy aliens" for most of the war. The light cast by my parents' story does not dispel the darkness of other Canadian stories. These too are "moments of truth".

A few years ago, I participated in a forty-day and -night peace vigil outside Litton Industries in Toronto, the company which was manufacturing the guidance system for the Cruise missile.

It wasn't easy to stand out there on some of the coldest days of the year. My face began to swell and blisters formed along my lips. Yet it was even more difficult to endure the verbal abuse shouted by some of the employees as they drove by our peace group on their way to and from work. "You bunch of Commies, you're wasting your time."

No, I said to myself, I am not a Commie. I am a Canadian. I wanted to say to them: "Let me tell you about Jack and Rita Leddy and how they spent their time in the war. That's why I'm spending my time here—standing and shivering for peace."

Memories serve us well when they present us with the possibility of making choices and promises that will make a difference in the future. The memories of Jack and Rita Leddy serve me well.

Notes

[1] Unfortunately the letters that were written between Jack and Rita Leddy during the war were lost during a move.

[2] The complete surgical records of Major John Edward Leddy are stored in the Manuscript Division of the General Archives of Canada in Ottawa.

[3] Learmonth, Professor J.R., "Note on a Visit to Medical Units in 21 Army Group", Journal of Royal Army Medical Corps, Vol. LXXXIV No. 5 (May 1945), p. 235.